curriculum
connections

Civil War
People

BROWN
BEAR
BOOKS

Published by Brown Bear Books Ltd

4877 N. Circulo Bujia
Tucson
AZ 85718
USA

First Floor
9–17 St. Albans Place
London N1 0NX
UK

© 2011 Brown Bear Books Ltd

ISBN: 978-1-936333-47-9

Managing Editor: Tim Cooke
Designer: Joan Curtis
Picture Researcher: Sophie Mortimer
Art Director: Jeni Child
Editorial Director: Lindsey Lowe

Library of Congress Cataloging-in-Publication Data

People / edited by Tim Cooke.
    p. cm. -- (Curriculum connections : Civil War)
Includes index.
 Summary: "In an alphabetical almanac format, includes biographies of significant individuals on both sides during the U.S. Civil War. Provides details of their lives and explains their contribution to the conflict"--Provided by publisher.
 ISBN 978-1-936333-47-9 (library binding)
 1. United States--History--Civil War, 1861-1865--Biography--Juvenile literature. 2. Leadership--History--19th century--Juvenile literature. I. Cooke, Tim, 1961- II. Title. III. Series.

E467.P436 2012
973.7092'2--dc22
[B]
                    2011005414

Picture Credits

Cover Image
Library of Congress

Alabama Department of Archives and History 86; Library of Congress 10, 15, 35, 44, 62, 70, 73, 75, 82, 104. National Archives 9, 16, 33, 38, 41 , 49, 51, 59, 61, 64, 69, 78, 93, 94, 99, 103; Robert Hunt Library 23, 24, 31.

Artwork © BrownBear Books Ltd

Printed in the United States of America

Contents

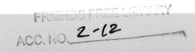

Introduction

Civil War **forms part of the Curriculum Connections series. Each of the six volumes of the set covers a particular aspect of the conflict: Home Front and the Economy; Behind the Fighting; Weapons, Tactics, and Strategy; Politics; Battles and Campaigns; and People.**

About this set

Each volume in *Civil War* features illustrated chapters, providing in-depth information about each subject. The chapters are all listed in the contents pages of each book. Each volume can be studied to provide a comprehensive understanding of all aspects of the conflict. However, each chapter may also be studied independently.

Within each chapter there are two key aids to learning that are to be found in color sidebars located in the margins of each page:

Curriculum Context sidebars indicate to the reader that a subject has a particular relevance to certain key state and national history guidelines and curricula. They highlight essential information or suggest useful ways for students to consider a subject or to include it in their studies.

Glossary sidebars define key words within the text.

At the end of the book, a summary **Glossary** lists the key terms defined in the volume. There is also a list of further print and Web-based resources and a full volume index.

Fully captioned illustrations play an important role throughout the set, including photographs and explanatory maps.

About this book

This book includes biographies of the most significant individuals to emerge on both sides during the Civil War. It provides concise details of their lives and explains their contribution to the conflict.

Many of the individuals featured were soldiers. The generation of officers who fought for the Union and the Confederacy had much in common. Many had formerly been colleagues in the Mexican War (1846–1848); most had been taught the same tactics by the same instructors at the U.S. Military Academy at West Point, Virginia. This volume highlights the battlefield successes that made commanders popular heroes—and the disasters that ruined careers.

There are also articles about the politicians who shaped the course of the war. They include Abraham Lincoln, whose election triggered the secession crisis in 1861, and Jefferson Davis, who once seemed likely to become president of the United States himself, but instead became the only president of the Confederacy.

Many individuals were inspired to become involved in the war in different ways. Women played a major role both as spies, like Rose O'Neal Greenhow and others who passed on secrets to both sides, and as nurses. Pioneers such as Clara Barton and Dorothea Dix influenced the development of modern professional nursing services in the United States. Meanwhile, writers and artists recorded both the details of the conflict and their own reaction to it.

Banks, Nathaniel P.

Nathaniel Banks (1816–1894) was one of President Abraham Lincoln's political appointees to the rank of general. He had no military experience, and his lack of skill proved costly for the Union. Banks led his troops to a series of defeats.

Curriculum Context

Some curricula ask students to study the emergence of the Republican Party and its effect on American politics.

Curriculum Context

Students should be able to describe how political appointments led to men with little military experience becoming officers on both sides early in the war.

Nathaniel Prentiss Banks was born in Waltham, Massachusetts, on January 30, 1816. He left school to work in a cotton factory. Later he studied law before becoming a politician. Elected to Congress in 1853 as a Democrat, he opposed the western expansion of slavery, and switched to the Republican Party in 1855. In 1858 he was elected governor of his home state. Lincoln needed the support of influential men when war began and gave them key military offices. In May 1861 the president appointed Banks major general of volunteers despite his lack of military experience.

Failed campaigns

In the summer of 1861 Banks and his men were routed by Confederate General Thomas "Stonewall" Jackson in the Shenandoah Valley, Virginia. On August 9, 1862, Banks came up against Jackson again at Cedar Mountain, Virginia. Banks and his men were beaten and the Union suffered 2,500 casualties. The military initiative in Virginia swung in favor of the Confederates and only Banks's friendship with Lincoln saved his job. Later campaigns reinforced Banks's poor military reputation. In May 1863 he led the Army of the Gulf against the Confederate stronghold at Port Hudson on the Mississippi. The Confederates successfully fought off the attack. Another Union assault on June 14 failed; the Confederates surrendered only after Vicksburg fell to the Union farther upriver. Banks fared no better in the Red River Campaign, and in 1865 he was removed from command. Banks returned to politics to serve in the House of Representatives.

Barton, Clara

Clara Barton (1821–1912) was a Union nurse remembered as the "Angel of the Battlefield." She was not a nurse by profession, and her only prewar medical experience was gained caring for her brother after he fell from a barn roof.

Clarissa Harlowe Barton worked as a teacher but later moved to Washington, D.C., to work at the Patent Office. Her war service began in April 1861, when she tore up sheets to make towels and bandages for the injured men of the 6th Massachusetts Regiment. Shocked to learn that many soldiers at the First Battle of Bull Run (July 21, 1861) died because of a lack of medical supplies, Barton advertised for donations and distributed the supplies. In 1862 Surgeon General William A. Hammond granted her a pass to travel behind the lines with army ambulances to nurse the wounded. The presence of a woman on the battlefield at the time was new and shocking.

Under fire

Barton nursed soldiers from both sides. She first nursed in the line of fire at the Battle of Cedar Mountain on August 9, 1862, where she tended the Union wounded and also helped at a field hospital for Confederate prisoners. At the Battle of Antietam in Maryland on September 17, 1862, Barton was nearly killed when a bullet passed through the sleeve of her dress, killing the wounded man she was attending. Her work during the Battle of the Wilderness, Virginia (5–7 May, 1864), won her national attention. After the war, Barton organized a program to search for soldiers missing in action and discovered the fates of 22,000 men. Later she established the American Red Cross, becoming its president in 1881. A tireless worker well into her 70s, Barton spent six weeks in Galveston, Texas, in 1900 helping victims of devastating floods.

Curriculum Context

Barton's story is a good example for students describing the role of women during the war.

Field hospital

A temporary hospital set up in tents or in adapted buildings near a battlefield.

Beauregard, Pierre G. T.

Beauregard (1818–1893) was one of the eight full generals of the Confederate army. He became a popular hero after commanding the bombardment of Fort Sumter in April 1861 and saw action in every major theater of the war.

Pierre Gustave Toutant Beauregard was born into a French Creole family in Louisiana. He attended the U.S. Military Academy at West Point, graduating second in his class in 1838. He served in the Mexican War (1846–1848) and was twice wounded.

When Louisiana seceded from the Union in January 1861, Beauregard resigned from the U.S. Army and was commissioned as the first brigadier general of the Confederacy. He was ordered to South Carolina, where he commanded the attack on the garrison at Fort Sumter in April 1861.

Military campaigns

Hailed as a hero across the Confederacy after the fall of Sumter, Beauregard took command of the Confederate army in northern Virginia. At the First Battle of Bull Run on July 21 Beauregard was second-in-command to Joseph E. Johnston, facing a Union army under his former West Point classmate, Irwin McDowell. Beauregard's network of spies in Washington provided valuable information on the Union forces, and his role in the battle earned him promotion to full general.

Beauregard moved west to command the Army of the Mississippi in March 1862. He was second-in-command to Albert S. Johnston in the Battle of Shiloh in April and took charge after Johnston was fatally wounded. His retreat from Shiloh and later withdrawal from Corinth angered President Davis, who fired him in June when Beauregard left his army without permission.

Curriculum Context

Beauregard was one of the leading military figures in the Confederacy, particularly in the early part of the war.

An excellent engineer and able commander, P. G. T. Beauregard was also vain and egotistical.

In August 1862 Beauregard returned to duty as the senior Confederate commander in Georgia and South Carolina. He organized the defense of Charleston until April 1864, when he transferred to help defend Richmond. After holding back a Union advance along the James River in May, he was assigned to overall command of the armies in Tennessee and Georgia in October 1864.

By January 1865 Beauregard was organizing the retreat through Georgia and the Carolinas. In February he ordered Charleston to be evacuated. In April, after the loss of Richmond and the Army of Northern Virginia, he was one of the senior figures who urged Davis to negotiate the surrender of the last Confederate forces to end the war.

After the war Beauregard returned to his home state of Louisiana, where he served as state adjutant general for several years.

Curriculum Context

You might be asked to describe the different attitudes toward surrender among Confederate officers and politicians.

Booth, John Wilkes

John Wilkes Booth (1838–1865) was a noted Shakespearean actor. He is mainly remembered as the man who assassinated President Abraham Lincoln to avenge the South less than a week after the Civil War ended.

Curriculum Context

Many curricula expect students to explain how the election of Lincoln alienated supporters of slavery.

John Wilkes Booth was born into a leading theatrical family on May 10, 1838, near Bel Air in the slave state of Maryland. The Booth home was 25 miles (40 km) south of the border with the free North. Booth was proslavery from an early age and thus became fervently anti-Lincoln.

After some early failures J. Wilkes Booth (as he was known on stage) made his name with the Richmond Theatre Company in Virginia in 1859. While in Virginia he became even more attached to the Southern way of life and joined the Richmond militia for a short time. As a militia officer he stood guard at the gallows during the hanging of the antislavery figure John Brown.

Although fiercely anti-Lincoln, John Wilkes Booth was a popular figure in Northern high society during the war. His good looks and acting talent gained him many admirers.

Booth was in great demand as an actor in Washington, D.C., during the war years. On November 9, 1863, President Lincoln saw Booth star in *The Marble Heart* by Charles Selby at Ford's Theatre.

As the war went on, Booth became increasingly upset by Confederate defeats and began to gain a reputation for bouts of wild behavior. In May 1864 Booth gave up acting. He dabbled in the oil business and may have become a Southern spy, smuggling quinine and other medicines to the Confederate army. In November Booth moved to Washington, where he and others devised various plots to kidnap the president. They intended to ransom Lincoln for the return of Confederate prisoners of war. However, their attempts all failed.

On April 9, 1865, Robert E. Lee surrendered to the Union. In a desperate, last-ditch show of support for the Confederacy, Booth decided to kill Lincoln.

The assassination

On the night of Good Friday (April 14) 1865 Lincoln attended a performance of *Our American Cousin* at Ford's Theatre. During the third act of Tom Taylor's play Booth entered the unguarded presidential box and shot Lincoln through the back of the head with a pistol. He leaped down onto the stage, shouting "Sic semper tyrannis! (meaning "So it always is with tyrants") The South is avenged!"

Despite having broken his left leg as he landed on the stage, Booth escaped on horseback. Twelve days later Union troops caught up with him on the farm of Richard Garrett near Bowling Green, Virginia. The soldiers set fire to the tobacco barn in which the assassin was hiding. Booth died in the ensuing gun battle, shot through the neck by Sergeant Boston Corbett.

Quinine
An anti-malaria medicine made from the bark of a South American tree.

Curriculum Context
Students might be asked to judge Lincoln's attitudes toward civil liberties and presidential power during the war. Is there any evidence that he was a "tyrant"?

Boyd, Belle

Belle Boyd (1844–1900) was one of the most famous Confederate spies of the Civil War. She was dubbed La Belle Rebelle (the beautiful rebel) by a French journalist after her exploits gained her worldwide celebrity.

Curriculum Context

You might be asked to describe the importance of espionage during the war.

Belle Boyd was born Maria Isabela Boyd in Martinsburg, Virginia (now West Virginia), in 1844. When Union forces occupied the town in 1861, 17-year-old Belle befriended officers, carefully noting comments about their plans, which were passed to Confederates in the field. She shot dead a drunken Union soldier in her family home, but was tried and acquitted. In May 1862, when she was staying at her father's hotel at Front Royal in Warren County, she discovered that a knothole in her bedroom floor allowed her to listen to Union officers in the parlor below. One night she overheard them discussing a plan to blow up key bridges around Front Royal to thwart an attack by Confederates led by General Thomas "Stonewall" Jackson. Belle jumped on a horse and rode 15 miles (25 km) through Union positions to tell Jackson, who responded by beginning his attack early. To thank her, Jackson made her an honorary member of his staff, with the rank of captain.

"Stonewall" Jackson

Read about Jackson on pages 60–62.

Captured by the Union

In 1862 Belle was arrested by the Union but released a month later. In 1863 she was imprisoned again and released suffering from typhoid. In 1864 she sailed for England. When the Union captured her ship, Belle charmed a Union officer, Sam Hardinge, into helping her. He was court-martialed and discharged, and the two later married in England. In 1865 she published her memoirs, *Belle Boyd in Camp and Prison*. In England she became an actress and then made her American stage debut in 1868. She continued her life on stage as a lecturer, entertaining audiences with her experiences.

Brady, Mathew

Mathew Brady (1823–1896) was the most famous photographer of the Civil War. His determination to use the new medium of photography to make a complete record of the conflict left thousands of memorable images.

Mathew Brady was born near Saratoga Springs, New York. Aged 16 he left home and moved to the town of Saratoga, where he enrolled as an art student under the portrait painter William Page. At the end of 1839 teacher and pupil traveled to New York City, where Page introduced Brady to the celebrated Samuel Morse. Morse had invented the telegraph, which would later make him world famous, but at this time he was better known as a painter and a professor of painting and design at New York University.

New technology

Morse had just returned from Paris, where he had been introduced to a pioneering photographic process—the daguerreotype—by its French inventor Louis Daguerre. Convinced that photography would become a sensation of the age, Morse set up a studio in New York and began giving classes in the daguerreotype

Curriculum Context

Photography is a good example of how technological innovation was changing life in the mid–19th century.

The "Wet-Plate" Process

A great technical advance in photography in the 1850s meant that Brady's photographic studios were able to turn out thousands of portraits a year. The early daguerreotype was a unique image created on a chemically treated copper or silver sheet that was then covered with protective glass. At the beginning of the 1850s, however, the "wet-plate" process was invented in Britain. In this method a light-sensitive liquid was used to fix a negative image to a glass plate. From this plate the photographer could make an unlimited number of positive prints and even enlargements. Alexander Gardner, a Scottish photographer and chemist, was a pioneer of the new process. When he became Brady's partner in 1856, the new process quickly supplanted the daguerreotype.

The Dead of Antietam

The aftermath of battle provided Brady's photographers with their greatest opportunity to record the reality of war. In the wake of the unprecedented carnage at the Battle of Antietam in September 1862 Brady opened his studio doors in New York to an exhibition of photographs entitled "The Dead of Antietam." Gruesome images of churned up, muddy fields strewn with broken and mutilated bodies shocked those who saw them. People were suddenly forced to open their eyes to the hideous brutality of warfare. Observers were moved to tears at what was for most of them their first glimpse of battle. The New York Times paid tribute to Brady, saying that he had brought home "the terrible reality and earnestness of war."

method. Brady leaped at the chance to study under Morse, working long hours in a department store to pay for his tuition. He found himself at the beginning of a brand-new profession.

Brady took full advantage of his opportunity. In 1844 he opened a daguerreotype studio on the corner of New York's Fulton St. and Broadway, and very quickly built up a large clientele for his high-quality portraits. Not content with commercial success, however, Brady also conceived a grand ambition to record the country's history through daguerreotype images of its most famous citizens. His growing reputation gained him access to past presidents such as John Quincy Adams and Andrew Jackson, as well as current politicians, including Henry Clay and Daniel Webster. In 1850 he published 24 such daguerreotypes in a volume entitled *Gallery of Illustrious Americans*. Over the next decade Brady became the most famous photographer in the United States. He opened lavish new premises at 10th and Broadway and eventually a studio in Washington, D.C.

Brady's grand scheme
At the outbreak of the Civil War Brady approached the Lincoln administration with a proposal to make a photographic record of the conflict. The idea was

approved, but Brady had to finance the ambitious undertaking himself. During months of preparation he assembled a large team of camera operators and technical support staff, and purchased and outfitted wagons with the bulky cameras and the chemicals essential to the photographic process. Brady then deployed his photographers throughout the war zone. From the First Battle of Bull Run in July 1861 to Lee's surrender to Grant in April 1865, Brady's photographers assembled an incomparable record of the terrible conflict that gave many civilians their first taste of war.

Brady's images were very much affected by the technical realities of photography at the time. Not only was the camera equipment heavy and cumbersome, but the exposure time for a photograph was measured in seconds, not milliseconds as today. This meant that the photographers could realistically only record static scenes. Groups of soldiers would be positioned in front of the camera or would hold a pose as they pretended to go about their their normal camplife activities. The picture they present is of the inevitable drudgery of military life during periods of relative calm.

Poverty and disappointment

Brady's huge and successful effort to create an enduring record of the Civil War brought him nothing but misery for the rest of his life. His professional ethics

A photographers' camp. Photographs in the 1860s had to be developed quickly, so photographers traveled around with darkroom wagons, like the one below.

A typical Brady photograph showing Union soldiers in camp. Photographs at the time could not capture action, so images of people are posed and static.

were criticized by some of his photographers, who felt it was unfair to have "Photograph by Brady" stamped on every photograph they took. No matter who took a photograph—and he took very few himself during the Civil War—if Brady owned it, it was a "Photograph by Brady." This practice went beyond putting his famous name to the work of his colleagues and employees. In his desire to create a comprehensive record of the war he tracked down and bought thousands of photographs taken by other photographers. Every time such photographs were reprinted, they also bore the credit "Photograph by Brady."

Worse than any bickering from his colleagues, however, Brady's Civil War activities ruined him financially. After the war there seemed nothing people wanted less than photographic reminders of those dreadful days. Brady had sunk into the project his entire fortune of $100,000, a huge sum at the time. When a market for his work failed to materialize, he was forced into bankruptcy. Finally, in 1875 Congress bought the entire archive for $25,000, but that sum was quickly eaten up by Brady's creditors. The United States' most celebrated photographer died nearly blind and penniless in 1896, but his work, now a national treasure, remains the greatest record of the war.

Bragg, Braxton

Braxton Bragg (1817–1876) was one of the Confederacy's most controversial generals. He owed his long stint in high command to the support of President Jefferson Davis, who blamed Bragg's failures on his subordinates.

An 1837 graduate of the U.S. Military Academy at West Point, Bragg fought with Jefferson Davis, the future Confederate president, in the Mexican War (1846–1848). In 1856 he resigned his army commission to be a sugar planter. When the Civil War broke out, Bragg was made a brigadier general. At the Battle of Shiloh, he served as a corps commander in the Army of Tennessee (then the Army of the Mississippi). Two months later President Davis appointed him the Army of Tennessee's top commander in place of Pierre G. T. Beauregard. Bragg held the post until December 1863.

Army command

At first Bragg did well. He restored discipline, then organized a remarkable campaign that took the army from northern Mississippi into Kentucky. After an inconclusive battle at Perryville on October 8, 1862, Bragg withdrew into central Tennessee. The retreat gave him a poor reputation, which dipped lower in December, when he attacked William S. Rosecrans' Union troops at the Battle of Stones River. Initial success was followed by defeat. When Rosecrans resumed the attack he outwitted Bragg, capturing Chattanooga, a crucial railroad center, almost without firing a shot. Bragg counterattacked. At the Battle of Chickamauga, he beat the Union forces and besieged Chattanooga, only to be repulsed two months later. After this defeat President Davis reluctantly removed him from command but made him his military adviser. Bragg was briefly recalled to military service by Lee, who took command of the army in 1865.

Mexican War

The United States fought Mexico from 1846 to 1848, following the U.S. annexation of Texas.

Curriculum Context

Students tracing the conduct of the war should be aware that various commanders had different strategies and tactics.

Brown, John

John Brown (1800–1859) was born into a New England abolitionist family and became one of the antislavery movement's most militant activists. He was hanged before the war and became a martyr for his cause.

Curriculum Context

John Brown's story will be of interest to students asked to describe the hardening attitudes for and against slavery before the war.

As a passionate enemy of slavery, John Brown worked closely with the free black community. He was a "conductor" on the "Underground Railroad," a secret series of safe houses for Southern slaves when they escaped to the North. In the mid-1850s his beliefs led him to violence. He saw slavery as a sin against God and resolved to use armed force and to encourage a slave uprising.

In 1855 Brown moved to Kansas with five of his sons to help prevent the territory from becoming a slave state. In 1856 proslavery settlers burned and looted the free-state community of Lawrence. Brown reacted savagely. On May 23 he and six followers murdered five proslavery men using swords at Pottawatomie Creek. After the murders Brown became a hate-figure for proslavers, who burned him out of his homestead. With financial help from Northern abolitionists he raided plantations in the neighboring slave state of Missouri.

Abolitionists

Members of the campaign to make slavery illegal.

Attack on Harpers Ferry

On October 16, 1859, Brown attacked the government armory at Harpers Ferry in western Virginia. He intended the raid to spark a slave revolt throughout Virginia and across the South. It failed. Brown and his men were surrounded in the fire house, and attacked by a company of U.S. Marines commanded by Colonel Robert E. Lee. Ten of Brown's men were killed and seven captured, including Brown. The authorities acted swiftly. Brown was tried and convicted. On December 2, 1859, he was hanged at Charlestown, Virginia.

Buckner, Simon Bolivar

Simon Bolivar Buckner (1823–1914) graduated from the U.S. Military Academy at West Point with Ulysses S. Grant in 1844. Buckner fought for the Confederacy in the Civil War, on the opposite side from his friend.

Buckner was born on April 1, 1823, in Hart County, Kentucky. In 1860 he became commander of Kentucky's state guard. Kentucky was a slave state and although Buckner was not a slave-owner he believed that states should decide whether to allow slavery or not. When the Civil War broke out, Kentucky resolved to remain neutral, but in September Kentucky officially endorsed the Union after the Confederate army invaded the state. Members of the militia rushed to join both sides. Buckner joined the Confederate army as a brigadier general.

Fighting the Union

In February 1862 Buckner attempted to lead a breakout from Fort Donelson, Tennessee, which was besieged by his old classmate Ulysses S. Grant. Buckner was left to surrender. Grant said his friend was the garrison's "most capable soldier" despite being third in rank. On October 8, 1862, Buckner led four brigades of Braxton Bragg's Army of Tennessee in the Battle of Perryville, the largest Civil War action in Kentucky. He also played a minor role in the biggest battle of the western theater, the Battle of Chickamauga, Georgia. The battle was a great victory for the Confederacy, but Buckner and others were critical of Bragg's leadership.

Buckner was a pallbearer at Grant's funeral in 1885. He entered politics and was elected governor of Kentucky as a Democrat in 1887 and ran for vice president in 1896. He outlived all other top-ranking Confederate generals, dying at age 90 in 1914.

Curriculum Context

Students studying the causes of the war should bear in mind that many people, particularly in the South, saw it as a conflict about states' rights as much as about slavery itself.

Surrender

Buckner was held in solitary confinement for five months before being swapped for a Union officer in a prisoner exchange.

Buell, Don Carlos

Don Carlos Buell (1818–1898) served with distinction in the Mexican War. When the Civil War began, he was considered one of the most promising Union officers and quickly rose to high command. However, he proved overcautious in combat.

Seminole War

The third war between the U.S. Army and Seminole in Florida was fought between 1855 and 1858.

Buell graduated from the U.S. Military Academy at West Point in 1841 and fought in the Seminole and Mexican wars. In November 1861 McClellan, the commander of the Union army, put Buell in charge of the Department of the Ohio. Five months later Buell's forces came to the aid of Ulysses S. Grant's beleaguered army at the Battle of Shiloh. He saved Grant from possible defeat on the evening of April 6, 1862, and greatly aided the Union counterattack the next day.

Buell's slow pace

After assisting in the capture of Corinth, Mississippi, during the Battle of Shiloh, Buell was ordered to march to Chattanooga, Tennessee, in early summer 1862. His pace was slow, partly because he repaired the Memphis & Charleston Railroad as he went, and partly because he was harried by Confederate cavalry raids.

The Confederate invasion of Kentucky forced Buell to fall back to defend the line of the Ohio River. He confronted the Confederates on October 8, 1862, and fought Braxton Bragg's army to a draw at the Battle of Perryville. Buell's failure to pursue the retreating Confederates led President Lincoln to relieve him of command in November. Lincoln was displeased by Buell's lack of aggressiveness and his political views. Buell was opposed to making the emancipation of slaves a war objective and to confiscating crops and other civilian property. An investigation into his actions was inconclusive, but Buell was not given any further command. He resigned from the army in June 1864.

Emancipation

Lincoln's Emancipation Proclamation made freeing the slaves a specific war aim in January 1863.

Buford, John

No Union general played a greater role in shaping the Battle of Gettysburg than cavalryman John Buford (1826–1863). Two of Buford's cavalry brigades started the fighting that developed into the largest battle of the war.

An 1848 graduate of the U.S. Military Academy at West Point, Buford served on the western plains, where he fought the Sioux and took part in the 1858 Mormon War in Utah.

After serving in the defense of Washington, D.C., in July 1862 he took command of a cavalry brigade in John Pope's Army of Virginia. Although wounded in the Second Battle of Bull Run, he recovered to serve as chief of cavalry of the Army of the Potomac during the Antietam and Fredericksburg campaigns in late 1862. In June 1863 he received command of the 1st Division, Cavalry Corps.

Glory at Gettysburg

The evening of June 30, 1863, Buford's division was posted north and west of Gettysburg in Pennsylvania. Although heavily outnumbered by Confederate forces, he prepared to hold the town until reinforcements arrived. Fighting on foot, his troopers fended off the Confederates for over three hours. A Union infantry corps arrived just as enemy pressure grew severe. Buford's correct pinpointing of the invading army's location, coupled with his skillful defense of the ridges west of the town on the next morning, helped ensure that the war's largest engagement was fought on terms favorable to the Union. This was his last contribution to the Union cause. In the fall of 1863 he fell ill with typhoid fever. On his deathbed he was promoted to major general, a rare honor. Backdated to July 1, 1863, the promotion recognized his great day at Gettysburg.

Mormon War

The Mormon War of 1858 was a standoff between the U.S. Army and Mormon settlers in Utah, whose laws did not fit with those of the United States.

Curriculum Context

Many curricula expect students to understand the progress of the Battle of Gettysburg; Buford's contribution was essential to the eventual Union victory.

Burnside, Ambrose E.

Ambrose Everett Burnside (1824–1881) took command of the largest Union army, the Army of the Potomac, in November 1862. He was replaced four months later following a disastrous march on the Confederate capital, Richmond.

Burnside graduated from the U.S. Military Academy at West Point in 1847 and served on the western frontier, where he was wounded in a fight with the Apache.

In May 1861 soon after the Civil War began, Burnside became colonel of the 1st Rhode Island Infantry and was assigned to defend Washington, D.C. By June he was commanding a brigade in the 2nd Division of Irvin McDowell's Army of Northeastern Virginia. He earned some credit during the First Battle of Bull Run on July 21, 1861.

Brigade

A brigade was a military unit of around 5,000 soldiers, made up of two to six regiments.

In August Burnside was promoted to brigadier general and sent to command an expeditionary force along the coast of North Carolina. Successes at Roanoke Island and inland at New Bern in mid-February 1862 led to his promotion to major general. In July Burnside sailed for Virginia with reinforcements to help General George McClellan's Army of the Potomac, which was fighting along the James River. Taking command of IX Corps, Burnside took part in the last actions of McClellan's Peninsular Campaign.

Peninsular Campaign

A Union campaign in spring and summer 1862 that attempted to capture Richmond via the Virginia Peninsula.

The Army of the Potomac moved back into northern Virginia in mid-September 1862, with Burnside now in command of both IX and I Corps. On September 14 this wing of the army opposed the Confederate invasion of Maryland at the Battle of South Mountain and on September 17 at the Battle of Antietam. At Antietam Burnside, commanding IX Corps on the Union left, was ordered to advance at 8:00 A.M. but took most of the day to force his way over a bridge at Antietam Creek— later called Burnside's Bridge.

Taking command

The Union claimed victory at Antietam when the Confederates withdrew to Virginia, but it was not a clear victory and led to McClellan's dismissal in November. Burnside had been criticized for ineffectiveness at Antietam, too, but he was now offered full command of the Army of the Potomac. He felt unequal to the post, but nevertheless he took control on November 9, 1862.

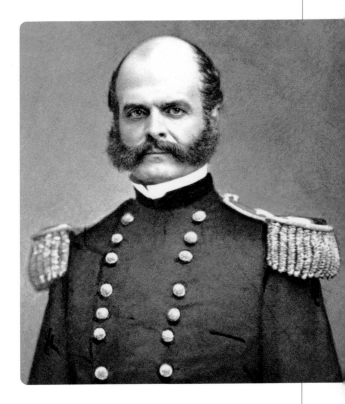

Burnside reorganized the army's six corps and cavalry into three Grand Divisions, Right, Center, and Left, and ordered a march on Richmond.

The "mud march" and demotion

Burnside's march was stopped at the Rappahannock River on December 13 as he attempted to drive Lee's Army of Northern Virginia off the heights dominating the town of Fredericksburg. The battle was a disastrous failure, and Burnside's attempt to keep his demoralized army fighting and marching through the mud and foul weather of January did more harm to his reputation. On January 25, 1863, he was replaced by Joseph Hooker.

Sent west to command the Department of the Ohio in March 1863, by August Burnside took a field command once more in charge of the small Army of the Ohio advancing from Kentucky into east Tennessee. On

Ambrose E. Burnside started the fashion for bushy side whiskers. They later became known as "sideburns" for their originator. This photograph was taken in 1861. In later life Burnside took to wearing his whiskers much longer.

September 3 he occupied the city of Knoxville, but by November 17 he was surrounded by Confederates under James Longstreet. The siege was only lifted on December 6 by the arrival of Sherman's Army of the Tennessee.

Replaced in his Ohio command after Knoxville, in April 1864 Burnside was transferred back to the Army of the Potomac, where he again took charge of IX Corps. Acting as a subordinate officer, Burnside did well in the battles of May and June that marked Grant's pursuit of Lee's army back toward Richmond: Wilderness, Spotsylvania, North Anna, and Cold Harbor. Only when he made an independent attack during the siege of Petersburg did he fail once again. The Battle of the Crater on July 30, heralded by the detonation of a huge mine, was in Grant's words "a stupendous failure. It cost us about 4,000 men ... all due to the inefficiency of the corps commander." Burnside's career did not recover. He was sent on leave and never recalled to service.

Battle of the Crater

When Union besiegers detonated a large mine to blow a gap in the Confederate defenses, the attackers became stuck in the resulting crater and were targeted by Confederate infantry.

The Burnside Carbine

Before the war, in 1853, Burnside left the U.S. Army temporarily to develop his own design of breechloading carbine, a type of light rifle. He set up a factory in Rhode Island, named the Bristol Firearms Company, and set about manufacturing his new rifle. Burnside's carbine had a unique cone-shaped cartridge. One complaint about Burnside's design was that the cartridge would occasionally stick in the breech (the rear of the barrel). However, it was a success, and the U.S. Ordnance Department bought 55,000. The Burnside was the third-most popular carbine used by the Union cavalry after the Sharps and Spencer designs. Burnside failed to keep the patent for his design, however, and was bankrupted by the venture.

Burnside's carbine was used by the Union cavalry during the war.

Butler, Benjamin F.

Benjamin Franklin Butler (1818–1893) was an abolitionist and politician who gained high rank in the Union army because of his connections. He did not achieve glory on the battlefield but dealt effectively with civilian unrest.

Butler was one of the North's most prominent "War Democrats," as Democrats who backed the Lincoln administration were called. As a combat leader he proved mediocre. He lost the war's first significant skirmish at Big Bethel, Virginia, on June 10, 1861. His offensive at Bermuda Hundred, Virginia, in May 1864 was a failure, and he squandered a fine opportunity to capture Fort Fisher, North Carolina, in December 1864.

As an administrator, however, Butler performed well. In April 1861 he put down the Baltimore Riot. The next month he refused to return a group of runaway slaves to their Southern owners, noting that they had been used in direct support of the Confederate war effort and were therefore "contraband of war," meaning prizes. Butler's decision became official Union policy on August 6, 1861, when President Lincoln declared that all contrabands were considered free.

New Orleans bound

Butler's greatest notoriety came in 1862, when he presided over New Orleans as commander of the occupying Union forces. He outraged Southerners by issuing his Woman's Order: any woman who insulted Union troops would be arrested and imprisoned as a prostitute. He became known as "Beast" Butler. After the war Butler returned to politics, this time as a congressman. In 1868 he served as a prosecutor in the impeachment trial of President Andrew Johnson and served as governor of Massachusetts from 1882 to 1884.

Baltimore Riot

On April 19, 1861, a brawl broke out between Confederate sympathizers and Union militia in Baltimore.

Curriculum Context

Students studying home life in the South under Union occupation could consider Butler's order and the resentment that it caused.

Chamberlain, Joshua L.

Joshua Lawrence Chamberlain (1828–1914) was one of the Union's military heroes during the Civil War. He fought with courage in many major battles. He was wounded six times—once near fatally—and had six horses shot from under him.

Joshua Lawrence Chamberlain was educated at Bowdoin College and Bangor Theological Seminary. In 1862, at age 34, he volunteered for military service and joined the 20th Maine Infantry as a lieutenant colonel.

A glorious career

At Fredericksburg Chamberlain and his men came under continuous Confederate fire for hours on the night of December 13, 1862. This was the beginning of Chamberlain's outstanding war. At the Battle of Gettysburg he led his regiment in defense of Little Round Top. For holding this key position in the face of enemy attacks, and for leading a bayonet charge when his men ran out of ammunition, Chamberlain was awarded the Congressional Medal of Honor in 1893.

During Union assaults on Petersburg in June 1864, Chamberlain's bravery so impressed Ulysses S. Grant that Grant promoted him to brigadier general in the field. Although wounded, Chamberlain soon returned to the front. On April 12, 1865, he was breveted major general and he had the honor of receiving the formal surrender of Robert E. Lee's men.

After the Civil War he refused a commission in the regular army. He served as governor of Maine and was president of Bowdoin College from 1871 to 1883. He spent his later years in business and was involved in the construction of a Florida railroad. He wrote about the war, including *The Passing of the Armies* (1915). He died in Portland, Maine, on February 24, 1914.

Medal of Honor

Abraham Lincoln introduced the Medal of Honor in 1861.

Breveted

To be promoted temporarily to a high rank, usually as a reward for success in action.

Chesnut, Mary B.

Mary Chesnut (1823–1886) wrote the most famous account of the Confederate home front. She organized and revised her journal entries into book form after the war, but the journal was not published until 1905, 19 years after her death.

Mary Boykin Miller was born on March 31, 1823, into a wealthy South Carolina planter family. Her father, Stephen Decatur Miller, had been a U.S. Representative and was elected governor of South Carolina in 1829, and a U.S. Senator in 1831. Mary Miller was educated at Mme. Talvande's French School for Young Ladies and became fluent in both French and German.

Mary married a young lawyer, James Chesnut Jr., in 1840. In 1858 James Chesnut was elected to the U.S. Senate. The couple moved to Washington, D.C., where they were close to Jefferson and Varina Davis—later to become the first family of the Confederacy. When the Republican Abraham Lincoln was elected president in 1860, James Chesnut resigned his Senate seat. The couple returned to South Carolina, where James worked on the state's ordinance of secession. As she would record in her journal, the Chesnuts had a lot of friends throughout Southern society as well as in the Confederate government.

Curriculum Context

Students might be asked to describe how individuals reacted to the coming conflict as the war approached.

Mary's journal

Early in 1861 Mary Chesnut began to keep a journal. She would keep writing it until June 26, 1865. Her husband's career placed her at excellent vantage points and she witnessed many of the key events as she accompanied her husband to the main sites of the Civil War. She was in Charleston for the bombardment of Fort Sumter, where she wrote, "I do not pretend to go to sleep. How can I? If Anderson [the Union garrison commander] does not accept terms—at four—the

Fort Sumter

The Confederate attack on the Union fort at Fort Sumter, in Charleston Harbor, on April 12, 1861, was the first military action of the war.

Curriculum Context

If you are asked to describe life on the Home Front in the South, it might be helpful to read Mary Chesnut's journal.

orders are he shall be fired upon.… At half past four, the heavy booming of a cannon. I sprang out of bed. And on my knees … I prayed as I never prayed before."

The Chesnuts soon moved to the new Confederate capital of Richmond. Mary's journal is a spirited account of the city's upper classes during the war. She wrote about "starvation parties" where hostesses served only water and about fine ladies selling clothes to buy food when the Confederate currency became worthless. Chesnut also wrote movingly about the turning tide of the war. When Atlanta fell to the Union in September 1864, Chesnut despaired: "Since Atlanta I have felt as if all were dead within me, forever.… We are going to be wiped off the earth."

After the war the Chesnuts were heavily in debt, and their old home was a shell. In the 1870s Mary revised her diary to make a book, but it was not published until after her death. The diary chronicled the changing fortunes of the Civil War. Chesnut worked hard in her revisions to turn the diary into a work of literature. Its description of Southern society and the roles both men and women filled make it an extremely important historical document, as does her account of the events of the Civil War unfurling without any certain idea of their outcome. She died at home in 1886.

Discussion with Davis

An extract from Chesnut's journal entry for April 17, 1861:

"In Mrs. Davis's drawing-room last night, the President took a seat by me on the sofa where I sat. He talked for nearly an hour. He laughed at our faith in our own powers. … We think every Southerner equal to three Yankees at least. We will have to be equivalent to a dozen now. … He believes that we will do all that can be done by pluck and muscle, endurance, and dogged courage. … And yet … there was a sad refrain running through it all. For one thing, either way, he thinks it will be a long war. That floored me at once. It has been too long for me already."

Cumming, Kate

Kate Cumming (1835–1909) cared for Confederate soldiers from after the Battle of Shiloh in April 1862 until the end of the war. Her diary, a moving account of Confederate hospital life, was published in 1866.

Kate Cumming was born in Scotland but emigrated with her family as a young child to North America. She was raised in Mobile, Alabama, where her father was a wealthy merchant.

Duty calls

In spring 1862 Cumming volunteered as a nurse, despite objections from her family. She had never been inside a hospital, but she believed that women from her social class should help the Confederate war effort. After the Battle of Shiloh, Tennessee, where casualties were heavy, Kate comforted the wounded. Based at the filthy Tishomongo Hotel, where most volunteers soon quit, Cumming was too busy to change her bloodstained dress for 10 days. In the fall of 1863 she worked in Chattanooga. Her role was managing the hospital and overseeing its laundry and kitchen.

Curriculum Context

Some historians believe that the South benefited from a tradition of women doing charitable work.

Kate's diary

Kate Cumming's journal was a detailed account of life in Confederate hospitals. It was published in 1866 titled *A Journal of Hospital Life in the Confederate Army of Tennessee*. Her experience convinced her of war's brutality.

Curriculum Context

Kate Cumming is a useful example of an individual who played a significant part in the war.

Later life

In 1874, Cumming moved to Birmingham, Alabama, where she taught school. In 1890 she published *Gleanings from Southland*, a revised version of her journal with a new, conciliatory tone toward the North. She died on June 5, 1909, in Birmingham.

Custer, George A.

General Custer (1839–1876) was a flamboyant Union cavalry officer who fought with distinction in the Civil War. He is best remembered, however, for leading his men to annihilation at the Battle of the Little Bighorn in 1876.

George Armstrong Custer was born in New Rumley, Ohio, in 1839 but moved to Monroe, Michigan. In 1857 he enrolled in the U.S. Military Academy at West Point and graduated four years later—at the bottom of his class of 34. Despite his poor placing, Custer had graduated at the right time. He reported for duty and was sent with dispatches to General Irvin McDowell, commander of the Army of the Potomac. There he was assigned to duty as lieutenant in the 5th Cavalry. On the day of his arrival he fought in the first major battle of the Civil War, at Bull Run on July 21, 1861.

Center of attention

From then on Custer was in the thick of the fighting, taking part in all but one of the battles fought by the Army of the Potomac. He gained a reputation for enthusiasm and bravery, and was promoted swiftly. By the war's end, aged only 25, Custer held a battlefield rank of major general. The "boy general," as he became known, also captured the public imagination with his striking image. He was dashingly good looking, with long golden hair set off by a bright red necktie and a custom-designed uniform dripping with gold braid. Neither his battlefield heroics nor his conspicuous appearance went uncriticized, however. Other generals noted that units under Custer's command suffered high casualties. His vanity and arrogance annoyed many.

Custer's talent for always being at the center of the action continued to the end of the war. He pursued and harried the Confederate commander Robert E. Lee

Dispatches

Written orders and reports between military commanders.

Curriculum Context

Custer and other commanders, like P. G. T. Beauregard in the South, were popular heroes during the war.

in the final days of the war and accepted the first flag of surrender in April 1865. He was also present at the surrender at Appomattox Court House.

After the war Custer sought further glory. In 1866 he was appointed lieutenant colonel of the newly formed 7th Cavalry in Kansas. He reveled in the 7th Cavalry's high-profile role, which was to batter the Plains Indians into submission and drive them onto reservations. Custer became a folk hero for his prowess as an Indian fighter. But when he failed to wait for supplies to be reloaded at Fort Harker and visited his wife, Custer was court-martialed. His one-year suspension was revoked when increased hostility by the Plains Indians meant he was needed. He rejoined the 7th Cavalry in Kansas in 1868.

General George Custer captured the first and the last battle flags of the Civil War.

In 1874, Custer led a party to investigate rumors of gold deposits in the Black Hills of South Dakota. The Sioux and Cheyenne who lived there were told to move to reservations. Instead, the tribes moved in the spring to join Sitting Bull's encampment on the Little Bighorn River in Montana. At the Battle of Little Bighorn on June 25, 1876, Custer and all 200 of his men died during an attack on a camp of Sioux and Cheyenne. The nation was stunned, and Custer was given a hero's burial at West Point. Later generations have been more critical of Custer and the mistakes that led him and his men to Little Bighorn.

Davis, Jefferson

Jefferson Davis (1808–1889) was the only president of the Confederate States. Before the war he was an influential senator, congressman, and secretary of war, and he had been widely seen as a possible future president of the United States.

Curriculum Context

Many curricula ask students to be aware of the careers of leading political figures such as Jefferson Davis.

Jefferson Finis Davis was born on June 3, 1808, in Kentucky. His family moved to Mississippi and did well in the cotton trade. Jefferson Davis grew up to believe devoutly in slavery and states' rights. He became the primary spokesman for Southerners on these issues in the prewar years, and even advocated the revival of the African slave trade. Davis was a well-known national figure; had the Southern states not left the Union, he might have become president of the United States. At one stage he saw himself as the only politician who could reconcile the troubled nation peacefully.

Marriage and family

Davis graduated from the U.S. Military Academy at West Point in 1828 and went on to serve on the frontier. He left the army in 1835 and married Sarah Knox Taylor. On the honeymoon both newlyweds came down with malaria, and Sarah died of the disease three months later. Davis suffered greatly from the loss. He rarely left his plantation, Brierfield, over the next 10 years. After this long widowerhood Jefferson married Varina Howell (1826–1905) in 1845 and, in the same year, was elected to Congress as a Democrat. Varina Howell Davis was a great influence on her husband and supported his politics. The couple had six children and a happy marriage.

Frontier

In the West, the U.S. Army protected settlers from Native Americans.

Military record

Davis returned to military duty to serve in the Mexican War (1846–1848) as colonel of a Mississippi mounted volunteer regiment. He became a hero at the Battle of

Buena Vista, where he sustained a serious wound in his foot. This military success further enhanced his political standing, and after the war he served as a senator for Mississippi and, from 1853 to 1857, as secretary of war under President Franklin Pierce.

Secession

When Mississippi left the Union on January 9, 1861, Davis made an eloquent farewell speech in the Senate in which he defended secession "upon the basis that the States are sovereign." His speech was emotional and, reportedly, "graceful, grave, and deliberate." One of his many friends, Senator James G. Blaine of Maine, later observed that "no man gave up more than did Mr. Davis" to pursue secession because "for several years he had been growing in favor."

Davis returned home to Mississippi, where he was appointed commander of the Mississippi militia. He wished to lead the Confederate army, but the provisional congress selected him as provisional president. He was inaugurated on February 18, 1861. He was later elected to the permanent post and inaugurated in Richmond, Virginia, on February 22, 1862.

A fitting president

Davis was an impressive president in many ways: imaginative, intelligent, and passionately committed to the cause of the Confederacy. There were few statesmen in the then seven Confederate states better qualified for the post. Davis was,

Sovereign
Empowered to rule itself.

Jefferson Davis photographed in 1860. After secession Davis hoped to lead the Confederate army. When, instead, he was chosen president, his wife wrote that he was "so grieved that I feared some evil had befallen our family."

Capture by the Union

Davis was captured on the night of May 10, 1865, near Irwinville in Georgia. He was not, as was later claimed by many people, dressed as a woman. When Union troops raided his camp, Davis attempted to flee. In his haste he had thrown over his shoulders his wife's rain shawl, which looked much like his own. Many mocking newspaper cartoons were published of Davis escaping in petticoats. In fact, when he knew all was up, he is said to have sat down by the campfire and said, "God's will be done." Davis was imprisoned for two years at Fort Monroe in Virginia. He wanted the publicity of a trial, but he never got one. The Union elected to let him go.

however, reserved and often severe in his manner. He could be indecisive yet stubborn, and he lacked humor and flexibility.

Six weeks after his appointment his new country was at war. Davis's personal role in the conduct of the war was great. He interfered continually in the War Department and went through six secretaries of war in four years. Davis made a fine decision in appointing Robert E. Lee to command the Army of Northern Virginia in May 1862. Lee also served as Davis's principal military adviser. Davis and Lee aimed to secure Confederate independence by inflicting a series of striking defeats on Union forces. Despite coming close, especially at Chancellorsville on May 2, 1863, it proved impossible. Davis also attempted to secure foreign military aid for the Confederacy. In fall 1861, following a diplomatic quarrel with the Union, the British government sent 11,000 troops to Canada to prepare for an invasion. Tempers cooled, and the invasion did not materialize.

Curriculum Context

Students may be asked to summarize Davis's strategy for Southern success in the war.

Finally, Davis hoped to win by holding on until the Union was overcome by war weariness. That almost happened in 1864 since Lee's army seemed too tenacious to destroy. In late summer 1864 President Lincoln's chances of reelection in November looked small. But then the city of Atlanta fell to the Union, and

General Philip Sheridan scored an impressive victory in the Shenandoah Valley. Lincoln was reelected, and their chances evaporated.

Favoritism

In his military appointments Davis has been criticized for relying too heavily on West Point training, even when the individual was inept. Davis clung to his favorites too long and could not work with people he disliked. For this reason Pierre G. T. Beauregard, a general who perhaps could have forged a victorious strategy for the Confederates, was relegated to a relatively minor role.

THE LAST DITCH OF THE CHIVALRY, OR A PRESIDENT IN PETTICOATS.

This Northern cartoon shows the arrest of Jefferson Davis, who was inaccurately rumored to have been disguised as a woman at the time.

Instead, Davis remained loyal to his friend Leonidas Polk, who made a poor general. While the president had, justly, been impressed with Braxton Bragg early in the war, he kept Bragg in field command for too long and later made the unpopular decision to bring him to Richmond as a principal adviser. Late in the war Davis, although rightly relieving Joseph E. Johnston from army command, made the unwise decision to elevate John Bell Hood in his place. Some historians believe that these three generals—Polk, Bragg, and Hood—made enough mistakes to doom the Confederacy.

After the war

Davis was imprisoned by the Union. After his release he and his wife Varina wrote long memoirs. They did not do well at the time and shed little light behind the scenes. Davis died on December 6, 1889, in New Orleans. Some Southerners in the late 19th century, blamed the president for the Confederacy's defeat. Many others, however, revered Davis's memory.

Curriculum Context

Students might be asked to evaluate Davis's achievements as president.

Dix, Dorothea

Dorothea Dix (1802–1887) was superintendent of women nurses for the Union army. She had previously spent 20 years as a reformer campaigning for improved conditions in mental hospitals and prisons, work she returned to after the war ended.

Dorothea Dix ran her own school in Boston for many years. Shocked by the inhumane living conditions she found on a visit to a Massachusetts prison in 1841, she began to campaign to expand hospital care for the insane and poor who were held in jails or poorhouses in Massachusetts. From 1843 through 1860 she traveled across the country to encourage the establishment of state mental hospitals. Thanks to her determination, Dix inspired many state legislators to set up state hospitals for the mentally ill.

Curriculum Context

Dorothea Dix is a good example of a woman who overcame 19th-century restrictions on women's role in society.

War post

The Union Secretary of War, Simon Cameron, accepted Dix's proposal to head a unit of women nurses in the Civil War. Dix, however, clashed repeatedly with Union army physicians, most of were against paying women to be nurses. They found allies in the unpaid women hospital volunteers. However, Dix succeeded in getting women accepted as paid nurses. But her strict rules—her nurses had to be plain women over 30 years old and had to wear brown or black clothes with no jewelry, curls, or other adornment—alienated her from the nurses. Her great determination, discipline, and dedication to her work were undisputed but she made many enemies and developed a reputation for being cranky and inefficient.

Curriculum Context

Dix's policies played a major part in the creation of the modern nursing profession.

In October 1863, the War Department removed many of her responsibilities. After the war Dix returned to her work campaigning for more humane treatment of the homeless and insane until her retirement.

Douglass, Frederick

Frederick Douglass (c. 1818–1895) was one of the leading human rights campaigners of the 19th century. A well-known abolitionist, he became the first African American to be given a high level appointment by the U.S. government.

Frederick Douglass, originally named Frederick Augustus Washington Bailey, was born into slavery in rural Maryland in 1817 or 1818. He was separated from his slave mother and knew nothing of his white father. At age eight he was sent to Baltimore to serve in the home of Hugh and Sophia Auld. Mrs. Auld began teaching him to read and write. When Hugh Auld discovered this, he put a stop to it—but too late. Douglass had learned the basics and from then on was able to teach himself. He did so to remarkable effect, in later life he became famous for the clarity of his writing and the eloquence of his speech.

After seven years in Baltimore Douglass was thrust back into rural slavery, where he was brutally treated. He vowed to gain his freedom. Six years later he escaped to the North and settled in New Bedford, Massachusetts, changing his birthname of Bailey to Douglass to escape slave hunters.

In 1841 Douglass spoke at an antislavery meeting where he impressed his listeners with his moving account of his experience of slavery. He was quickly taken up by the impassioned abolitionist William Lloyd Garrison and soon became much in demand as a lecturer for the Massachusetts Anti-Slavery Society. His fame spread with the publication of the first of his three autobiographies in 1845. Three years later he undertook a successful lecture tour of Great Britain. With the money he earned, he was able to buy his freedom and start an antislavery newspaper.

Curriculum Context

In parts of the Deep South it was forbidden to teach slaves to read and write, because it was feared it would encourage them to rebel against slavery.

Curriculum Context

Students describing the conditions of slavery could consult the *Narrative of the Life of Frederick Douglass* for material.

Political campaigner

Douglass believed in political action as well as moral persuasion to end slavery. He reacted angrily to the Fugitive Slave Act of 1850. "The only way to make the fugitive slave law a dead letter," he thundered, "is to make half a dozen or more dead kidnappers!" He also raised passions with the catchphrase "Who would be free must himself strike the first blow!" In 1859, however, he condemned John Brown's raid.

Instead, he threw his support behind Abraham Lincoln's 1860 presidential campaign, hailing the Republican victory as "an antislavery triumph." Douglass remained an influential adviser to the president throughout the Civil War, arguing in favor of the emancipation of the slaves. He recruited black soldiers to serve in the Union armies, and two of his own sons fought in the renowned 54th Massachusetts regiment.

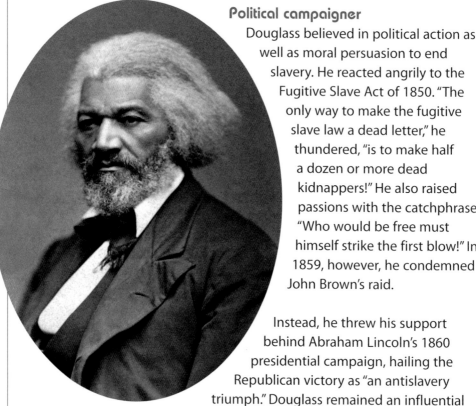

This photograph of Frederick Douglass was taken after the Civil War in about 1879.

After the War

After the war Douglass continued to campaign for full civil rights for African Americans. He was an active campaigner for women's suffrage and he worked to ensure the rights of freedmen and women in the period of Reconstruction. He held numerous public offices and in 1872 became the first African American to be nominated for the position of vice president. He was nominated without his knowledge and did not campaign. He died on February 20, 1895 after attending a meeting of the National Council of Women in Washington, D.C.

Early, Jubal A.

Jubal Early (1816–1894) was an eccentric but respected Confederate general who was reputedly willing to fight anyone, anywhere. "Old Jubilee" never surrendered and went abroad at the end of the war, although he later returned to the United States.

Jubal Anderson Early was an 1837 graduate of the Military Academy at West Point. He resigned his commission for a time to begin a career as an attorney and politician. He returned to serve in the Mexican War (1846–1848) as a major in charge of volunteers. In 1861, Early entered Confederate service as colonel in the 24th Virginia Infantry. He was promoted to brigadier general after First Bull Run and served with the Army of Northern Virginia from 1862 to 1864. He developed a reputation as a hard fighter and one of Robert E. Lee's best division commanders.

A hard fighter

The first day of the Battle of Gettysburg was one of Early's best days of the war. After the battle he criticized his superior officer, Richard S. Ewell, for failing to attack the Union position on Cemetery Hill. Following Ewell's removal during the 1864 Virginia campaign, Early took command of II Corps. His forces were defeated and dispersed in the Shenandoah Valley by Union troops under Philip H. Sheridan. Lee relieved Early of his command following this embarrassment.

After the war Early lived in Mexico and Canada before returning to Virginia to practice law. He continued to fight the Civil War with pen and printing press. Early became a leading advocate of the Lost Cause: the idea that the Confederates' cause had been noble but doomed. Early's war memoirs are remarkable for their insights and biting comments. He died in Virginia in 1894, an "unreconstructed Rebel" to the end.

Lost Cause

The Lost Cause created a view of the prewar South as a harmonious and happy society, destroyed by the industrialized and resentful North.

Ewell, Richard S.

The career of Richard Stoddert Ewell (1817–1872) began with promise but ended in controversy. Ewell was a respected Confederate cavalry officer who took over from Thomas "Stonewall" Jackson but failed to live up to his predecessor.

Ewell attended the U.S. Military Academy at West Point, graduating in 1840. He was breveted for gallantry during the Mexican War (1846–1848), and resigned his U.S. Army commission in May 1861 after the outbreak of war. Ewell rose quickly through the Confederate officer corps. After service at First Bull Run (Manassas) and in the Shenandoah Valley campaign Ewell served in the Army of Northern Virginia's II Corps. He lost a leg during the Second Bull Run campaign in August 1862 and could not return to service until the following May, after he had been equipped with a wooden leg. Following Thomas "Stonewall" Jackson's death, Ewell took command of II Corps.

Failure to attack

On the outskirts of Gettysburg at the end of fighting on July 1, the first day of the battle, Ewell made his most famous decision: not to attack fortified Union positions on Cemetery Hill. Some of his subordinate officers, and many historians have criticized Ewell for not living up to the aggressive standard of Jackson. Ewell remained in command of II Corps, but criticism and the effects of his leg wound reduced his efficiency. He lost his composure at a key moment during the Battle of Spotsylvania and then bungled an attack on part of the Union army. Robert E. Lee moved him into an administrative position, from which he emerged in 1865 to participate in the retreat to Appomattox. He was captured with part of the army's rear guard. After the war Ewell lived as a farmer in Tennessee and died a wealthy man in 1872.

Farragut, David G.

Farragut (1801–1870) was a Union naval hero. He was already 60 when the Civil War broke out, but his daring actions led to the capture of the ports of New Orleans (1862) and Mobile (1864). In 1866 he became the first American admiral.

David Glasgow Farragut was born in 1801 near Knoxville, Tennessee. As a child he was unofficially adopted by Captain David Porter of the U.S. Navy. At age nine he enlisted on Porter's frigate USS *Essex* as a midshipman and saw action during the War of 1812. For the next 50 years Farragut served in the navy. Those times were mainly peaceful, and in 1861 he was due for retirement after a long but uneventful career.

Born in the South and married to a Virginian, Farragut decided he was going to "stick to the flag" and moved North with his family in the Civil War. He became the Union's most celebrated naval officer.

Capture of New Orleans

Farragut's career, far from being over, was about to take off in a spectacular way. Although a Southerner by birth, he was a staunch Unionist. In January 1862 he was given command of the squadron tasked with capturing New Orleans, the largest city in the Confederacy. Under cover of darkness on April 24, 1862, Farragut's fleet blasted its way past the heavily defended forts Jackson and St. Philip, flanking the Mississippi below New Orleans. He lost only three vessels in the action. The next day Farragut forced the surrender of New Orleans, which was soon occupied by Union troops. The capture of New Orleans was a turning point in the war. Farragut was made a rear admiral of the U.S. Navy, the first man to hold that rank.

Battle of Mobile Bay

After the capture of New Orleans, Mobile, Alabama, was the only significant Confederate port left on the Gulf of Mexico. On August 5, 1864, Farragut led an attack on Mobile Bay, which was protected by sea mines (then called torpedoes) as well as by Fort Morgan and a Confederate fleet. Blinded by the smoke of battle, Farragut climbed the rigging of his ship and had himself lashed to the mast so that he could see to direct operations. Shortly afterward one of his ships struck a torpedo and sank. This disaster brought the fleet to a potentially fatal standstill in front of the big guns of Fort Morgan. Farragut's cry— "Damn the torpedoes! Go ahead!"—rallied the Union fleet, which went on to win the battle decisively.

This was Farragut's last action of the war. As a national hero, he was awarded the rank of admiral in 1866. He died in 1870.

Forrest, Nathan B.

Nathan Bedford Forrest (1821–1877) was one of the South's finest cavalry commanders. During the war he fought for the Confederacy throughout the Deep South, rising from the rank of private to lieutenant general.

Forrest had very little formal education and no military training before the Civil War broke out in 1861. He was a self-made man who had supported his family from his teenage years and prospered as a plantation owner and slave trader.

Tennessee planter

Within days of Tennessee voting to secede on June 8, Forrest enlisted as a private in White's Mounted Rifle Company. The state governor persuaded him to personally finance a new cavalry unit. Forrest first saw action during the defense of Fort Donelson, Tennessee, in February 1862. When the fort surrendered, he refused to let himself be captured and led his men to safety through Union lines. Promoted to full colonel in March, he took command of the 3rd Tennessee Cavalry. After the Battle of Shiloh he fought as part of the Confederate rear guard. During the retreat to Corinth, Mississippi, he was seriously wounded for the first time.

Rear guard
A small unit that protects the back of a much larger group as it retreats.

Cavalry commander

When he recovered, Forrest was given command of a cavalry brigade with which he launched a raid, attacking and overwhelming the Union garrison at Murfreesboro, Tennessee, on July 18. He was promoted to brigadier general three days later. During the winter of 1862–1863 Forrest continued raiding into western Tennessee and toward the Union garrison at Nashville. He also supported Braxton Bragg's advance into Kentucky in September and covered his retreat the following month.

This 1868 cartoon depicts Forrest as a butcher in allusion to the part he played in the massacre of black troops at Fort Pillow.

In April 1863 Forrest and a small force of cavalry pursued a Union column of 1,500 mounted infantry under Abel Streight. At Cedar Bluff, Alabama, Forrest called for Streight's surrender. Deceived by the Confederate commander's self-confident demand, Streight surrendered his entire force to Forrest's cavalry, which in fact numbered barely 600 men.

Forrest also distinguished himself at the Battle of Chickamauga. Despite contributing to the Southern victory, however, Forrest quarreled with Braxton Bragg and offered to resign. Instead, President Jefferson Davis gave him an independent command in western Tennessee and in December promoted him to the rank of major general.

Massacre at Fort Pillow

On April 12, 1864, during Forrest's capture of Fort Pillow, Tennessee, there were high casualties among the Union garrison of mostly black troops. Union soldiers claimed that Forrest's men had massacred defenders after they surrendered. The action was a major blemish on Forrest's reputation. In January 1865 he was given command of all the cavalry in Alabama, Mississippi, and eastern Louisiana. The next month he was promoted to lieutenant general. In his last campaign he was defeated at Selma, Alabama and finally surrendered at Meridian, Mississippi, on May 9.

Postwar career

After the war Forrest became a leading organizer in the newly formed Ku Klux Klan. His involvement with it, his career as a slave trader, and his actions at Fort Pillow show an unpleasant side to a man who was such an effective soldier.

Fort Pillow

Forrest's men were said to have killed some 500 Union defenders in cold blood, including the majority of the fort's African Americans.

Ku Klux Klan

The Klan was formed by veteran Confederate soldiers and waged a campaign against Reconstruction.

Frémont, John C.

John Charles Frémont (1813–1890) had a dazzling but inconsistent career. He was a hero before the war for leading a series of expeditions to the West. But severe Union defeats under his command dented his reputation.

Born in Georgia, Frémont led a number of expeditions to the far West. By the end of the 1840s he had played a significant role in taking California from Mexico and was a popular hero. When California became a state in 1850, Frémont was elected one of its first senators. He amassed a fortune from the 1849 gold rush.

Abolitionist

Despite being a Southerner, Frémont held strong antislavery views. At the start of the Civil War Lincoln gave Frémont command of the Department of the West based in St. Louis, Missouri. Without consulting Washington, D.C., Frémont declared Missouri's slaves free. Lincoln repudiated the order and in July 1861 relieved Frémont of his command.

Curriculum Context

Why might Lincoln have countermanded Frémont's order? Wasn't it a good thing to free Missouri's slaves?

Up against Stonewall

In March 1862 Frémont was given command of the Mountain Department in West Virginia, bringing him head-to-head with Confederate General Thomas "Stonewall" Jackson in the Shenandoah Valley. His troops took such a mauling that he was demoted, but he refused to serve under his former subordinate, John Pope. This marked the end of Frémont's military career. In 1864 he challenged Lincoln for the presidency as a breakaway Radical Republican. The scheme fizzled out before election day, and apart from a spell as governor of Arizona Territory from 1878 to 1883, Frémont took no further part in political life. Meanwhile, he had lost his fortune through rash speculation in railroads. Frémont died an almost forgotten figure in 1890.

Radical Republican

The Radicals were a group of Republicans who believed that Lincoln was too moderate in his approach to slavery, which they wanted abolished without compensation to slave owners.

Gibbon, John

John Gibbon (1827–1896) was a dedicated Union officer who was repeatedly in the thick of the fighting throughout the war. His book *The Artillerist's Manual* (1860) was highly regarded and used by both sides in the conflict.

Curriculum Context

Students could use Gibbon's family as an example where relatives fought on different sides in the war.

Gibbon grew up in the South. After graduating from the U.S. Military Academy at West Point in 1847, Gibbon served in the Mexican War (1846–1848) and in Florida. From 1855 he was an artillery instructor at West Point, where he wrote an influential artillery manual. On secession, he chose to fight for the Union, although three of his brothers fought for the Confederates. Initially Gibbon served as chief of artillery but soon switched to the infantry, where he quickly gained a reputation as an able leader and a resolute campaigner.

Iron Brigade

At the Second Battle of Bull Run (Manassas) Gibbon led a Midwestern brigade against Confederate General Jackson's seasoned veterans. The "Iron Brigade" was known for its hard fighting and featured in all the great battles of the eastern theater. Gibbon was wounded at Fredericksburg and again at Gettysburg while resisting Pickett's Charge. He was one of the Union generals chosen to accept the formal surrender of Robert E. Lee's Army of Northern Virginia on April 12, 1865.

Postwar career

After the war Gibbon enjoyed more military success in command of the U.S. 7th Infantry, on the western frontier. In June 1876 Gibbon's regiment was first to arrive on the scene at Little Bighorn after General George A. Custer's entire command had been killed in an attack on a Sioux encampment. Gibbon's regiment had to bury Custer's men. Gibbon retired from the army in 1891 and died five years later.

Gordon, John Brown

A native of Georgia, John Brown Gordon (1832–1904) was the model citizen–soldier. His complete lack of prewar military training did not hamper his swift rise through the ranks in the Confederate army during the Civil War.

Gordon began his Confederate service in 1861 by raising a company of volunteer infantry known as the "Raccoon Roughs." When the governor of Georgia declined his services because the state had filled its volunteer quota, Gordon took his men to Alabama to enlist. As colonel of the 6th Alabama, Gordon took part in the Seven Days' Battles around Richmond in June 1862, earning a reputation for fearlessness in combat.

Earning stars

Gordon's reputation increased following the Battle of Antietam (Sharpsburg). His regiment occupied the center of the sunken road that later became known as Bloody Lane, resisting Union attacks. Gordon suffered four wounds, the last a head wound that almost killed him. Shortly after Antietam he was awarded his brigadier general's star. He rose through the ranks of the Army of Northern Virginia, serving as a brigade commander at Gettysburg. He planned and carried out a brilliant attack at the Battle of the Wilderness in May 1864. His abilities, combined with casualties among Confederate General Robert E. Lee's officers, led to his promotion. By April 1865 Gordon was in command of over half of Lee's remaining soldiers. He surrendered along with Lee at Appomattox on April 9, 1865.

After the war Gordon returned to Georgia, where he was elected U.S. senator three times and governor of Georgia once. He was a driving force behind the Confederate veterans' movement and wrote an influential memoir of his wartime service.

> **Curriculum Context**
>
> Gordon's stand at Antietam was a turning point of the battle.

Grant, Ulysses S.

Ulysses Simpson Grant (1822–1885) was the Union's most outstanding general. As general-in-chief of the Union army, he directed the defeat of the Confederacy in 1865. After the war he served two terms as president of the United States.

Grant graduated from the U.S. Military Academy at West Point in 1843 and went on to serve in the Mexican War (1846–1848). His early career as a soldier was spoiled by rumors of drunkenness, and he resigned his captaincy in 1854. Civilian life proved just as unsuccessful. After several failed business ventures, in 1861 Grant was working as a clerk in the family store in Galena, Illinois.

When war broke out in April 1861, Grant offered his services to the War Department. He was initially refused but, with the aid of a supportive senator, was given command of the 21st Illinois Volunteers in June. In July he was promoted to brigadier general of volunteers and given command of the District of Southeast Missouri, with headquarters at Cairo, Illinois.

First success

Grant's first major success was on the Cumberland River at Fort Donelson, Tennessee, in February 1862. The defeat and capture of the Confederate garrison brought him to the notice of the Northern press and public for the first time. His brilliant battle tactics and refusal to accept any terms except unconditional surrender thrilled the Union public.

The success was shortlived, however. Grant commanded Union forces at the Battle of Shiloh, along the Tennessee River on April 6, 1862. It was only with the aid of William T. Sherman and substantial reinforcements that he avoided defeat after a

Curriculum Context

Many curricula ask students to assess the influence of Ulysses S. Grant in the military victory of the Union.

Unconditional surrender

A surrender in which terms are not negotiated but are wholly imposed by the victors.

Ulysses S. Grant at Cold Harbor, Virginia, in June 1864. Grant was famous for his lack of formality, in both his behavior and his style of dress.

Confederate attack under Albert S. Johnston took him completely by surprise. This near-failure and a row with his superior, Henry W. Halleck, took Grant from field command for a while. He was reinstated with the support of President Abraham Lincoln, who commented, "I can't spare this man—he fights." Grant's aggressiveness in taking the war to the enemy was already winning favor in Washington, D.C. It was in stark contrast to the timid leadership shown by Union General George B. McClellan trying to chase Confederate General Robert E. Lee in Virginia.

Victory at Vicksburg

Given command of the Army of the Tennessee in October 1862, Grant's next objective was Vicksburg, the key to Confederate control of the lower Mississippi River. In a combined operation with Union navy gunboats Grant advanced on Vicksburg and laid siege

Curriculum Context

Students might be asked to evaluate the advantages and disadvantages of more aggressive command over a more cautious approach.

Grant at Appomattox

Grant described his feelings on the day of Robert E. Lee's surrender at Appomattox on April 9, 1865.

"When I had left camp that morning I had not expected so soon the result that was then taking place, and consequently was in rough garb. I was without sword, as I usually was when on horseback on the field, and wore a soldier's blouse for a coat, with the shoulder straps of my rank to indicate to the army who I was. When I went into the house I found General Lee. We greeted each other, and after shaking hands took our seats. ... What General Lee's feelings were I do not know. As he was a man of much dignity, with an impassable face, it was impossible to say whether he felt inwardly glad that the end had finally come, or felt sad over the result, and was too manly to show it. Whatever his feelings, they were entirely concealed from my observation; but my own feelings, which had been quite jubilant ... were sad and depressed. I felt like anything rather than rejoicing at the downfall of a foe who had fought so long and valiantly, and had suffered so much for a cause, though that was, I believe, one of the worst for which a people had ever fought, and one for which there was the least excuse."

to it. The city finally surrendered on July 4, 1863, to huge rejoicing in the North. The victory was a turning point in Grant's career. He was rewarded with a promotion to major general.

On October 16, 1863, Grant took command of all Union forces from the Mississippi River to the Appalachian Mountains. He immediately went to assist the Union army besieged at Chattanooga, Tennessee. Victory there during the battles of November 23–25 secured Grant the personal thanks of his president and a move by Congress to award him the specially revived rank of lieutenant general. He went to Washington, D.C., in March 1864 to receive both his promotion and the post of general-in-chief of all Union armies.

Grant's strategy was to wear down the Confederate armies and at the same time finish off the Southern economy by destroying its rich farm lands. In May 1864 he traveled with the Army of the Potomac toward Robert E. Lee and Richmond. The six-week Overland

Curriculum Context

Students might be expected to be able to summarize Grant's overall strategy for the defeat of the Confederate armies.

Campaign was a bloody affair that resulted in 60,000 casualties. Despite the high cost in men and repeated tactical reverses, Grant kept moving forward.

Defeat of the Confederacy

The Army of the Potomac forced Lee's army back to Petersburg and besieged it for 10 months. Grant's subordinate, William T. Sherman, marched through Georgia from Atlanta to the sea, destroying Confederate supply lines and cutting a swath of destruction through the state. By the time Sherman reached the coast, his troops had caused $100 million in damage. Sherman then turned north and desolated the Carolinas. On April 2, 1865, Lee withdrew from Petersburg, and Richmond had to be evacuated. After a seven days' fight Grant cornered Lee at Appomattox, where he accepted Lee's surrender. Lee acknowledged the generosity of Grant's surrender terms.

Hailed as the nation's hero, Grant was promoted to full general in 1866. In 1868 he was elected the 18th U.S. president, serving two terms that were marred by several scandals. Grant's reputation was restored by the publication of his memoirs, which are among the finest written about the Civil War. They were completed only a week before his death in 1885.

Terms
Grant allowed the Confederates to leave and let them keep their horses and mules to take back to their farms; he also provided food stores for the defeated troops and forbade his own men from celebrating their victory over an enemy who were once again their fellow Americans.

Ulysses S. Grant (standing center in front of a tree) with his staff in June 1864 in Virginia during the Overland Campaign. By this time Grant was general-in-chief of all Union forces.

Greeley, Horace

Horace Greeley (1811–1872) was the founder and editor of the influential Tribune newspapers and the leading Northern journalist of the Civil War period. He championed many causes but is best remembered for his antislavery editorials.

Horace Greeley became apprenticed to a printer in Vermont at the age of 15. At 20 he set off for New York City with $10 in his pocket. After a succession of newspaper jobs he set up a printing firm with a friend. In 1841 he launched the newspaper that made his name: the *New York Tribune*. The paper gained popularity through the 1840s and 1850s. At its peak during the Civil War it had a circulation of 300,000. It was the most influential paper of the time. As the war started, Greeley came out against slavery but later supported compromise with the Confederacy.

"Prayer of Twenty Million"

Greeley's most famous editorial, on August 20, 1862, addressed President Abraham Lincoln on behalf, he said, of 20 million Northerners. In it Greeley demanded the immediate freeing of all Confederate slaves. Lincoln's reply, that his aim was to restore the Union—with or without slavery—became one of his most quoted statements of the war. The next month, Lincoln issued his preliminary Emancipation Proclamation, and Greeley's editorial is credited with encouraging him.

Political ambition

In 1872 Greeley ran for president but lost by a landslide to the incumbent president, Ulysses S. Grant. Greeley's wife had died just days before the election, and he also felt keenly his failure and the attacks of the press. He died on November 29, 1872, some said of a broken heart. Thousands of people joined his funeral procession on Fifth Avenue, New York.

Greenhow, Rose O'Neal

Rose O'Neal Greenhow (1817–1864) was one of the Confederacy's most successful spies. Her position as a society hostess in the Union capital of Washington, D.C., allowed her to gain valuable military information from her influential contacts.

Rose O'Neal Greenhow came from a wealthy slave-owning family in Maryland. She moved to Washington, D.C., after her marriage, where she became known for her beauty and her brilliant mind.

Spy network

Greenhow set up a Confederate spy network in the Union capital. Her work helped secure the Confederate victory at the First Battle of Bull Run (Manassas). She got hold of a copy of Union General Irvin McDowell's battle plans and passed them on to the Confederate commander Pierre G. T. Beauregard.

Arrest and imprisonment

The Union counterespionage chief Allan Pinkerton became suspicious of Greenhow and placed her under house arrest on August 23, 1861. She and her daughter " Little Rose" were sent to Washington's Old Capitol prison in January 1862. On her release in June 1862 Rose was exiled to the Confederacy, where she was given a hero's welcome. Soon afterward the Greenhows traveled to Europe to raise support for the Confederate cause. While in England in 1863 Greenhow published an account of her life, which became a bestseller. In September 1864 she sailed home on the British blockade-runner *Condor*. When the ship ran aground during a storm, Greenhow, fearing arrest, insisted on going ashore in a lifeboat. The lifeboat capsized, and Rose drowned, weighed down by the gold sewn into her dress. Her contribution to the Confederate cause was recognized with a military funeral.

Pinkerton
After the war, Pinkerton set up a famous detective agency.

Blockade-runner
A fast ship designed to smuggle goods through the Union naval blockade of Confederate ports.

Halleck, Henry W.

Major General Henry Wager Halleck (1815–1872) was general-in-chief of the Union army for two years. He was a talented administrator, but his understanding of field affairs was poor. Halleck was replaced by Ulysses S. Grant in March 1864.

Halleck graduated from the U.S. Military Academy at West Point in 1839. He served in the Mexican War (1846–1848) and later taught military strategy and tactics. His book *Elements of Military Art and Science* was standard reading for army officers when the war broke out. He was considered to be one of the leading intellects in the U.S. Army, and was charged with bringing order to the Union forces in Missouri, Arkansas, Illinois, and western Kentucky. One of his subordinates in the western theater was Ulysses S. Grant. Halleck claimed credit for Grant's successful seizure of Forts Donelson and Henry, Tennessee, in February 1862. This success earned him command of the Department of Mississippi in March 1862.

Poor field command

Grant's ability as a field commander outshone Halleck's. At the bloody Battle of Shiloh, Grant snatched victory from the jaws of defeat. Four days later Halleck arrived and called for reinforcements, amassing 100,000 troops. He advanced on Corinth, Mississippi, a town occupied by 70,000 Confederates. Despite having more men, Halleck advanced so cautiously—covering just 20 miles (32 km) in three weeks—that the enemy escaped. This was the only campaign in the field that Halleck led. Lincoln realized his shortcomings and made him general-in-chief, a Washington-based job that used Halleck's administrative ability. In this role he continued to annoy Grant with his interference. In the spring of 1864 Grant replaced Halleck, and Halleck was made chief of staff.

Hancock, Winfield Scott

Winfield Scott Hancock (1824–1886) was a professional soldier and one of the best corps commanders in the Union army. Union General Ulysses S. Grant said that Hancock's men "always felt that their commander was looking after them."

After graduating from the U.S. Military Academy at West Point in 1844, Hancock fought in the Mexican War of 1846–1848. He was made brigadier general of volunteers in the Union army shortly after the Civil War began, and led a brigade of the Army of the Potomac during the Peninsular Campaign of 1862. During the Battle of Antietam (Sharpsburg) he took over the 1st Division, II Corps, when its commander was killed. Hancock led the 1st Division during the battles of Fredericksburg and Chancellorsville. He was given command of II Corps in late May 1863.

Role at Gettysburg

Hancock played a key role at Gettysburg. Army commander George G. Meade ordered him to decide whether the Army of the Potomac should retreat after the death of Union General John F. Reynolds. Hancock decided to fight. He rallied the fleeing troops and helped organize a defensive position around Cemetery Hill, where the Confederate advance was halted. On the third day at Gettysburg he was seriously wounded and was invalided out of field command for nine months. He returned to active duty as corps commander for Grant's Richmond campaign in May 1864, fighting at the battles of the Wilderness and Spotsylvania. By the fall II Corps was entrenched in the Siege of Petersburg. Hancock's wound forced him to give up his corps command and return to Washington, where he commanded the military divisions covering the capital. He stayed in the army after the war. In 1880 he made an unsuccessful bid for the presidency as a Democrat.

Peninsular Campaign

An unsuccessful Union attempt to capture the Confederate capital, Richmond, by fighting up the Virginia peninsula.

Curriculum Context

If you are asked to explain the key moments that made Gettysburg such an important battle, you should focus on Hancock's decision. What might have happened had he decided to retreat?

Hill, Ambrose P.

Ambrose Powell Hill (1825–1865) was one of the best divisional commanders in Robert E. Lee's Confederate Army of Northern Virginia. In the later stages of the war, however, he was promoted beyond his ability.

Ambrose P. Hill was an 1847 graduate of the U.S. Military Academy at West Point. He gave his allegiance to Virginia when the war broke out in 1861, accepting a command in the Confederate army. He rose quickly to division command in Robert E. Lee's Army of Northern Virginia.

"Light Division" commander

Hill's division earned the nickname "the Light Division" for its fast marching and aggressive attacks. During the Confederate invasion of the North in 1862 Hill's men made a forced march on September 17 to the Antietam (Sharpsburg) battlefield, arriving in time to deliver a devastating counterattack to a part of the Union Army of the Potomac. When Lee reorganized his army in May 1863 after the death of "Stonewall" Jackson, he looked to Hill to command his newly created III Corps.

As a division commander Hill had been a great success, but as a corps commander, he surpassed the limits of his effectiveness. The lingering effects of a venereal disease contracted at West Point left him irritable and prone to bouts of illness. He was unequal to the task of corps command at Gettysburg and in the following Virginia campaigns. At the Battle of Bristoe Station in October 1863, for example, he led his corps into a disastrous ambush by Union troops. In the absence of other qualified generals, however, Hill stayed in corps command until he was killed by a Union sniper in the chaos of the final Union breakthrough at Petersburg, Virginia, on April 2, 1865.

Forced march

A march that is so long or made so quickly that it would normally exhaust the soldiers making it but which is militarily necessary.

Ambush

A surprise attack launched by hidden troops who have been lying in wait.

Hood, John Bell

John Bell Hood (1831–1879) rose quickly through the ranks of the Confederate army. He was an effective, aggressive division commander but proved disastrous in command of the Army of Tennessee, which he led to near-destruction.

Hood graduated from the U.S. Military Academy at West Point in 1853. After a number of rapid promotions early in the war, Hood attained his brigadier general's star on March 6, 1862, and took command of the renowned Texas Brigade. It made a bold charge at the Battle of Gaines' Mill on June 27, 1862, which earned the Army of Northern Virginia its first victory. This performance confirmed Hood's reputation as a hard fighter. The Texas Brigade made another successful attack at the Battle of Antietam (Sharpsburg). Hood was promoted to major general the following month.

Division command

Hood continued to distinguish himself. His division played a key part in Longstreet's assault on the second day of Gettysburg, where Hood was badly wounded. At the Battle of Chickamauga, he was wounded again and had his right leg amputated. He returned to the field in February 1864 as a corps commander in the Army of Tennessee led by General Joseph E. Johnston.

In the campaign to defend Atlanta the overcautious Johnston was removed from command, and Hood replaced him. Hood launched four major offensives to break the Union siege of Atlanta, but failed. Hood's aggressive style caused heavy casualties in his army. In November he invaded Tennessee, where he destroyed what was left of his army in disastrous battles at Franklin and Nashville. Hood was relieved of command at his own request. After the war Hood lived in New Orleans, where he died from yellow fever in 1879.

Yellow fever

An infectious disease transmitted by mosquitoes.

Hooker, Joseph

Joseph Hooker (1814–1879) was a Union general who rose to command the Army of the Potomac in late 1862. Shortly after a crushing Union defeat at the Battle of Chancellorsville in May 1863 Hooker asked to be relieved of his command.

Born in Hadley, Massachusetts, on November 12, 1814, Joseph Hooker graduated from the U.S. Military Academy at West Point in 1837. He fought bravely in the Mexican War (1846–1848) and reached the rank of lieutenant colonel. In 1853 Hooker resigned from the army to run a farm in California.

When the Civil War broke out in 1861, Hooker returned east and took over as brigadier general of volunteers, leading troops in the Peninsular Campaign (April 4–July 1, 1862) against Richmond. He showed great bravery in the Battle of Williamsburg on May 5, 1862, and was promoted to major general of volunteers from this date. When he appeared in a report of the battle as "Fighting Joe," the name stuck, although Hooker himself never liked his nickname. Hooker again showed courage at Second Bull Run (Manassas) in August 1862. He commanded I Corps in the Army of the Potomac at Antietam in September 1862 and was wounded in the foot.

Despite Hooker's prowess in battle, his private life was less controlled. He drank heavily and could be disagreeable and critical of his superiors.

Commanding the Army of the Potomac

In December 1862 President Lincoln promoted Hooker to command of the Army of the Potomac following the army's defeat at Fredericksburg under General Ambrose E. Burnside. In the letter of promotion Lincoln praised Hooker's fighting abilities but also

Curriculum Context

Do you think it mattered what Hooker was like in person if he was such a successful general?

criticized his outspoken opinions—in particular Hooker's idea that the country should be ruled by a military dictator after the war.

At the Battle of Chancellorsville in May 1863 Hooker proved badly indecisive. He was outgeneraled by Robert E. Lee and his Confederate Army of Northern Virginia, who defeated the Union forces despite being outnumbered two to one. Hooker stayed in command for a short while, but resigned on June 28 when he was refused reinforcements. He was replaced by General George G. Meade.

Hooker went on to serve ably in the Battle of Lookout Mountain, Tennessee, in November 1863 and under William T. Sherman in Georgia. After the war Hooker was passed over for army promotion. He retired following a stroke in 1868 and died in 1879.

Curriculum Context

Chancellorsville is a good example of how superior Lee's tactical abilities were to those of many of his Union opponents.

On taking command of the Army of the Potomac in December 1862, Joseph Hooker boasted that he would "whip Bobby Lee."

Jackson, Thomas J.

One of the greatest Confederate commanders, Thomas "Stonewall" Jackson (1824–1863) was famous for his brilliant tactics and bold strikes against Union forces. His career was cut short by his untimely death after the Battle of Chancellorsville.

Thomas Jonathan Jackson was born on January 21, 1824, in Clarksburg, Virginia (now West Virginia). He was orphaned at an early age and was brought up by relatives. Jackson had little formal education until he entered the U.S. Military Academy at West Point in 1842. After graduating in 1846, he fought in the Mexican War (1846–1848), during which he was promoted three times for bravery.

Virginia Military Institute

After the Mexican War Jackson left the army, finding peacetime service unrewarding. In 1851 he was appointed professor of artillery tactics and natural philosophy at the Virginia Military Institute (VMI) in Lexington, where he remained for 10 years. He became a Presbyterian, and his faith had a profound influence on him for the rest of his life—he was sometimes called "Deacon Jackson."

Jackson had several eccentricities; for example, he imagined that one side of his body weighed more than the other and so often walked or rode with one arm raised to keep his balance. During his time at VMI he married twice. His first wife, Elinor Junkin, died in childbirth. In 1857 he married Mary Anna Morrison, who bore him his only surviving daughter, Julia, in 1862. In 1859 Jackson witnessed the execution of the abolitionist John Brown, when he accompanied a group of VMI cadets to stand guard at the hanging. He later wrote that he was so moved by Brown's plight that he petitioned for his pardon.

Presbyterian

A member of a Protestant church that follows the doctrines of John Calvin.

Petition

To make a written request to the authorities.

Jackson joined the Confederate army when the Civil War started out of loyalty to his home state, Virginia. He earned his nickname of "Stonewall" at Bull Run (Manassas) in July 1861, the first major battle of the war. As his brigade stood firm in the face of a Union onslaught, a fellow officer, General Barnard Bee, rallied his troops by pointing out the conduct of Jackson and his brigade: "There is Jackson, standing like a stone wall!" For his actions Jackson was promoted to major general in October 1861.

"Stonewall" Jackson became a hero in the Confederacy for his aggressive tactics and the speed with which he moved his troops from place to place.

Valley campaign

In spring 1862 Jackson led a campaign in the Shenandoah Valley, during which he defeated Union generals whose combined strength was several times his own. His orders were to keep Union General Nathaniel P. Banks from joining forces with General George B. McClellan, who was fighting the Peninsular Campaign. During the six-week campaign Jackson's diversionary tactics succeeded brilliantly. The speed with which Jackson's troops were able to march earned them the nickname of Jackson's "Foot Cavalry."

Diversionary

Intended to distract enemy troops from a larger action.

Jackson then joined Robert E. Lee, who had taken command of Southern forces in Virginia and reorganized them into the Army of Northern Virginia. In the ensuing Seven Days' Campaign of June 1862 Jackson became slow and ineffective, probably due to physical exhaustion. He soon recovered, however, and at Second Bull Run (Manassas) he marched with 20,000 men over 50 miles (80 km) in two days, destroying the Union supply base at Manassas Junction on August 27. At the battles of Antietam (Sharpsburg) on September

Curriculum Context

Students discussing the most successful military leaders of the Confederacy should consider including both Lee and Jackson.

17 and Fredericksburg on December 13 his troops fought hard, making a great contribution to a string of Southern victories. In October 1862 Jackson was promoted to lieutenant general, and Lee gave him command of II Corps of the Army of Northern Virginia. The two men worked well together: Jackson said he trusted Lee so much he would follow him blindfolded.

Battle of Chancellorsville

In May 1863 Jackson won his greatest victory at Chancellorsville, Virginia. Lee sent him on a wide flanking march to attack the right wing of Joseph Hooker's Union army from the rear, which Jackson accomplished with devastating effect. But the battle had a tragic aftermath. Returning home from a scouting mission on the evening of May 2, Jackson's party was mistaken for enemy troops, and he was shot by his own men. The wound was not fatal, but his arm had to be amputated. He contracted pneumonia and died eight days later, on May 10, 1863. Jackson's death was a bitter loss for the Confederate cause and particularly for Robert E. Lee, who mourned: "I know not how to replace him."

A drawing entitled "Three Heroes" showing three of the great Confederate commanders: In the center is General Robert E. Lee, flanked by Stonewall Jackson (right) and J. E. B. Stuart (left).

Johnson, Andrew

Andrew Johnson (1808–1875) was elected vice president in November 1864. The following April President Lincoln was assassinated, and Johnson became president. He faced the daunting task of reconstructing the troubled nation.

Born in Raleigh, North Carolina, Andrew Johnson came from a poor family and had very little schooling. He was apprenticed to a tailor at the age of 13. Moving to Greeneville, Tennessee, in 1826, he began a tailoring business of his own. He married Eliza McCardle in 1827, and with her help, learned to read and write and then went on to educate himself further. His business prospered, and he used his ambition, drive, and gift for public speaking to enter Greeneville politics, becoming a town alderman in 1828 and then mayor in 1830.

A national figure

In 1843 he entered Congress as the Democratic Party's representative for Tennessee. He remained in Congress until 1853 and then returned to Tennessee as governor. He was elected to the Senate in 1857. In his prewar career he spoke out against the plantation owners who dominated politics in Tennessee and the rest of the South. In the great 1850s debate over whether or not slavery should be extended into the new territories, Johnson supported the Southern belief that it should. Although he upheld the institution of slavery, he remained pro-Union and refused to support Southern secession even after Tennessee seceded in May 1861. Johnson was the only senator from a seceded state to remain at his post in Washington, D.C.

Pro-Union Democrat

During the war the Republican President Lincoln recognized Johnson's political usefulness as a pro-Union Southern Democrat. In March 1862, after Union

Alderman
A senior official in town or city government.

Curriculum Context

It might be useful to study the reasons for Johnson's decision to remain loyal to the Union.

President Andrew Johnson came into bitter conflict with Congress. He favored a lenient approach toward the defeated South, while Congress wanted to seize the chance to radically reshape the Southern states and grant political rights to the freed slaves.

forces had occupied central Tennessee, Lincoln appointed Johnson military governor of the state. Johnson's staunch work for the Union in the face of persistent local hostility, led to his selection as Lincoln's running mate in 1864. Lincoln was reelected, and Johnson became vice president. He had been in the office for only six weeks when Lincoln's assassination on April 14, 1865, resulted in Johnson becoming the new president.

Presidency and impeachment

Johnson tried to continue Lincoln's policy of clemency toward the defeated Confederacy. However, the Radical Republicans, who now dominated Congress, opposed him. Their differing views on how to reconstruct the South turned into a bitter political struggle.

On May 29, 1865, Johnson announced a pardon for many former Confederates before Congress was in session. He firmly believed he had the support of the people, and went on to use his presidential veto to thwart several bills passed by Congress. On March 2, 1867, despite Johnson's veto, Congress passed a Reconstruction Bill and the Tenure of Office Bill, which limited the president's freedom to remove officials. In defiance of this Johnson dismissed Secretary of War Edwin M. Stanton—a Radical Republican—in August 1867. On February 28, 1868, Congress voted to impeach Andrew Johnson on charges of misconduct centering on the firing of Stanton. Johnson's Senate trial took place between March 5 and April 11, 1868. The charges did not stand up to scrutiny, and the president was acquitted. He continued in office until the end of his term in 1869, but he was almost powerless. Johnson later made two attempts to return to public office before winning a Senate seat in March 1875. He died suddenly on July 31.

Johnston, Albert S.

At the beginning of the Civil War Albert Sidney Johnston (1803–1862) was one of the most promising Confederate generals. His friend President Jefferson Davis saw his decision to fight for the Southern cause as a sure sign of victory.

Johnston graduated from the U.S. Military Academy at West Point in 1826. During the Mexican War (1846–1848) he led the 1st Texas Rifles as colonel for the Republic of Texas, and his success led him to return to regular U.S. Army service. He became colonel of the 2nd Cavalry in 1855, and after a campaign into Utah against the Mormons in 1857 he was promoted to the brevet rank of brigadier general. Johnston was serving in California when the Civil War broke out in April 1861.

Johnston resigned from the U.S. Army after Texas seceded. President Jefferson Davis gave him command of all Confederate forces west of the Appalachian Mountains to the Mississippi River. Johnston held a defensive line in Kentucky until January 1862. However, his subordinates' defeat at the Battle of Mill Springs on January 19 and the loss of Forts Henry and Donelson in February forced him to abandon Kentucky and most of Tennessee to the Union.

Fatal wound

Johnston's reputation was tarnished by these failures, but he rallied his forces in northern Mississippi and launched a counteroffensive into southwest Tennessee in April. He took the Union army of General Ulysees S. Grant by surprise in an attack at Pittsburg Landing on the Tennessee River on April 6. The Battle of Shiloh was Johnston's last fight. In the afternoon, directing his troops near the front line, he was shot in the leg. He ignored the wound and bled to death. His death was a great loss felt by his army and the whole Confederacy.

Brevet rank
A rank awarded temporarily as a reward for distinguished service in action.

Counteroffensive
An advance launched in response to an enemy offensive.

Johnston, Joseph E.

Joseph Eggleston Johnston (1807–1891) was the only general to command, at one time or another, every major Confederate army. He was valued for his skill as a defensive strategist although he was sometimes thought too cautious.

A graduate of the U.S. Military Academy at West Point in 1829, Johnston took part in the Second Seminole War in Florida and the Mexican War (1846–1848). In 1860 he was appointed quartermaster general of the U.S. Army and was the highest-ranking officer to resign when war started. He entered Confederate service as a brigadier general, then the highest rank in the Confederate army. He was placed in command of all forces in Virginia following the First Battle of Bull Run (Manassas). In May 1862 he was wounded at the Battle of Fair Oaks (Seven Pines). Robert E. Lee replaced him.

Relationship with Davis

In November 1862 Confederate President Jefferson Davis put the recuperating Johnston in command of the Department of the West. Johnston oversaw two Confederate armies. Johnston and Davis disagreed over how to defend Vicksburg from the Union and Davis blamed Johnston after the town surrendered on July 4, 1863. Davis grew impatient with Johnston's defensive strategy at Atlanta, Georgia, in May 1864 and relieved him of command. Atlanta fell to the Union anyway, and Johnston returned to duty in March 1865 at Robert E. Lee's request. He had initial success at Bentonville, North Carolina, but he had too few men and soon realized it was hopeless to resist further. On April 17 Johnston met with Sherman to negotiate surrender.

After the war Johnston served as a congressman and then as commissioner of railroads. He died of pneumonia on March 21, 1891.

Quartermaster
The officer in charge of supplying a military force.

Atlanta
Atlanta fell to Union troops in August 1864, after a four-month siege.

Lanier, Sidney

The poet and musician Sidney Lanier (1842–1881) fought in the Confederate army. His novels and poetry published after the war expressed a sense of loss and a nostalgia for the Old South, which echoed the feelings of many Southerners.

Sidney Lanier grew up in a well-to-do family, playing a variety of musical instruments at an early age. When Georgia seceded from the Union in 1861, Lanier enlisted as a private in the Macon Volunteers.

War service

Lanier served alongside his younger brother Clifford, three times refusing a commission so as not to be separated from him. He carried his flute with him, entertaining his comrades and finding some solace from the conflict in music. Lanier fought in the battles of Fair Oaks (Seven Pines) and Drewry's Bluffs, and in the Seven Days' Battles around Richmond. He and his brother also survived the Battle of Malvern Hill. The brothers were finally separated in 1864 when they served on ships running the Northern blockade. Clifford's ship was captured, and he was sent as a prisoner of war to Point Lookout, Maryland. There he contracted tuberculosis, which eventually killed him.

Lanier was positive about rebuilding the nation after the war. In his first novel, *Tiger Lilies* (1867), he described war as a "strange, enormous, terrible flower" and hoped that "this seed might perish in the germ, utterly out of sight and life and memory." Lanier faced financial problems until 1874, when he became a flutist in the Peabody Symphony Orchestra in Baltimore. He won national recognition in 1875, with the publication of his poems "The Symphony" and "Corn." Much of his poetry was linked to life in the South and the hardships facing his fellow Southerners.

Curriculum Context

Students describing soldier life should bear in mind the importance of diversions such as music in camp.

Curriculum Context

You might find it interesting to read some of Lanier's poems. How much do they reveal about how Southerners saw the war?

Lee, Robert E.

Confederate General Robert E. Lee (1807–1870) endures in the American memory as perhaps the country's most beloved and revered soldier. From May 1862 he commanded the most famous Confederate army, the Army of Northern Virginia.

Born into a prominent Virginia family on January 19, 1807, Robert Edward Lee was the son of General "Light Horse Harry" Lee, one of George Washington's subordinates in the Revolutionary War (1775–1783). His career after the Revolution was marred by scandal and debt, and Robert's boyhood home, Stratford Hall, passed to another Lee relative. Robert moved with his mother, Ann Hill Carter Lee, to a small home in Alexandria, Virginia. His father died soon after in 1818.

An appointment to the U.S. Military Academy at West Point in 1825 set the course of Lee's life. He flourished, and graduated in 1829 with the distinction (still held) of being the only graduate to finish without a single demerit for misconduct. After West Point he was commissioned into the Corps of Engineers. As a lieutenant and then a captain of engineers, Lee worked on improving various fortifications and harbors.

Marriage and Mexico

In June 1830 Lee married Mary Ann Randolph Custis, which connected him by marriage to the family of George Washington (Mary was the daughter of Martha Washington's grandson) and cemented his position in the Virginia aristocracy. The marriage was a happy one and produced seven children.

At the outbreak of the Mexican War (1846–1848) Lee accompanied General Winfield Scott's expedition to Vera Cruz in Mexico, earning battlefield distinction for scouting and staff work. He was promoted for bravery on three occasions and returned to the United States in 1848 as one of the nation's premier young officers and a protégé of Scott, who became the commanding general of the U.S. Army. Lee served for three years as the superintendent of West Point and in 1855 received a permanent promotion to lieutenant colonel. Transferred to Texas, he served as second-in-command of a cavalry regiment until the outbreak of the Civil War in 1861. Scott called Lee to Washington, D.C., and on April 18 offered him command of United States armies forming against the rebellious Southern states.

Agonizing decision

The split between North and South, combined with his expected role in suppressing the forthcoming rebellion, put Lee in a very difficult personal position. Lee's family owned slaves and was one of Virginia's oldest and most eminent. When Virginia joined the Confederacy in April, Lee reached the agonizing, but for him unavoidable, decision to resign from the U.S. Army. He did so on April 20, citing in a letter to Scott his inability to raise his sword against his family and state. Lee was immediately placed in command of Virginia's army and navy. When Virginia's forces came under the control of the Confederate government, Lee was appointed brigadier general, one of the five original Confederate general officers.

Scott

Scott's career is described on page 87.

Curriculum Context

Lee's dilemma was typical of that faced by many Americans at the start of the war: whether to remain loyal to the country or to their state and family.

Robert E. Lee leads his troops at the Battle of Chancellorsville, Virginia, in May 1863. Many consider this battle, in which Lee defeated a Union army twice his size in a series of daring maneuvers, to be his greatest tactical victory.

A postwar photograph of Robert E. Lee. After the war ended, he became president of Washington College, in Lexington, Virginia. He set a great example by refusing to express any bitterness and working hard for the country's reconciliation.

After a short, unsuccessful field command in western Virginia and an inspection tour of coastal fortifications in South Carolina and Georgia, Lee returned to Richmond to become chief military adviser to Confederate President Jefferson Davis. After Joseph E. Johnston was wounded in fighting against an advancing Union army, Lee assumed command of Confederate forces defending Richmond. His creation of the Army of Northern Virginia in June 1862 cemented his path to military glory.

Lee's tactics

Upon assuming command, Lee began to use the tactics that would frustrate Northern hopes in the eastern theater of war for the next two years. Most of Lee's battles involved an attempt to fix the enemy in position and at the same time maneuver parts of his army to outflank and destroy his opponent. Lee used a decentralized style of command in which he issued his subordinates overall guidance and left them to accomplish battlefield victory.

In June 1862 Lee immediately took the initiative, beating General George B. McClellan's Union Army of the Potomac in the Seven Days' Battles and saving the Confederate capital of Richmond, Virginia. After dealing with McClellan, he turned his attention to John Pope's Union Army of Virginia, marching north and crushing it at the Second Battle of Bull Run (August 29–30, 1862).

This string of victories compelled Lee to attempt his first invasion of Northern territory in September 1862. He suffered a tactical stalemate at the hands of George B. McClellan at the Battle of Antietam on September 17 and had to retreat back to Virginia. Lee then dealt the Union stinging defeats at Fredericksburg (December 1862) and Chancellorsville (May 1863). His aggressive methods continued to result in victories, but at a high cost in casualties.

Gettysburg and after

Ever mindful of growing Union numerical superiority and the limits of Confederate manpower and resources, Lee determined once again to invade Northern territory in June 1863, hoping to gain military and political advantage. At Gettysburg on July 1–3 he suffered a major defeat, an expensive setback that forever robbed the Army of Northern Virginia of its offensive striking power. From then until the end of the war Lee was constrained to fighting on the defensive, aiming to prevent any Union victory in the east and in this way to influence the upcoming 1864 Union presidential election.

From May 1864 Lee waged a titanic campaign against the adversary who finally defeated him, Union General Ulysses S. Grant. Grant's Overland Campaign in Virginia slowly wore down the Army of Northern Virginia and reduced both it and its general to shadows of their former selves. After besieging Richmond and Petersburg from the summer of 1864, Grant's army broke through the Petersburg fortifications in the first days of April 1865, forcing Lee to evacuate the Confederate capital and leading to his surrender at Appomattox Court House on April 9, 1865.

Postwar years

For the rest of his life Lee served as an example of reconciliation and leadership for all Americans, working to heal the wounds of civil war. He was elected president of Washington College in Lexington, Virginia, in August 1865. His personal example revived the fortunes of the small school (it was later renamed Washington and Lee University in his honor).

After his death in 1870 Lee was mythologized by Southern "Lost Cause" advocates, but he is also loved and honored worldwide as both a great soldier and a good man, one of history's outstanding commanders.

Curriculum Context

In summer 1864 Lincoln was highly unpopular; many people hoped that his opponent in the presidential election, George McClellan, would defeat him and make peace with the Confederacy.

Lost Cause

According to the Lost Cause myth, the Southern armies fought for a noble cause but were doomed to defeat by the North's greater resources and technological superiority.

Lincoln, Abraham

The Civil War threatened the survival of the Union like no other event in the history of the United States. The crisis called for an exceptional leader, and the nation found that leader in the 16th president, Abraham Lincoln (1809–1865).

Lincoln was an unlikely choice for president. He was born in a one-room log cabin in Hardin County, Kentucky, on February 12, 1809. His father, a poor frontier farmer, could provide his son with little formal education. Lincoln's mother died when he was nine, and the family moved to Indiana and then to Illinois. He served briefly in the Illinois militia in 1832. Despite his lack of schooling, Lincoln educated himself to a high level with borrowed books and participated in a local debating society.

In 1834 Lincoln was elected to the Illinois legislature as a member of the Whig Party. He served four terms while studying law and settled in the new state capital, Springfield. By the 1840s he was a successful lawyer. In 1842 he married Mary Todd from a wealthy Kentucky banking family. Four years later he was elected to the House of Representatives. As a congressman he opposed the United States' war with Mexico. This was unpopular, and Lincoln was not reelected. He returned to his law practice in Springfield but remained active in Whig politics.

Republican candidate

The Kansas–Nebraska Act of 1854, which potentially opened up the Northern territories to slavery, outraged Lincoln. He joined the new Republican Party, which was opposed to the westward expansion of slavery, and in 1858 the party nominated him for the Senate. Lincoln's performance in seven public debates against his Democratic opponent in Illinois, Stephen A.

Whig Party

A party founded in 1834 to promote manufacturing, commercial, and financial interests.

Curriculum Context

Some curricula expect students to understand the circumstances in which the Republican Party was created and how it differed from the Whigs.

Douglas, brought him to national prominence. During this campaign Lincoln summed up the crisis the nation was facing: "A house divided against itself cannot stand. I believe this government cannot endure permanently half slave and half free." When the Republican convention met in May 1860, Lincoln won the nomination for president. In the November election he received 39.8 percent of the popular vote and won the election with 180 of the 303 electoral votes.

Taking the nation to war

In the slaveholding states not one electoral vote was cast for Lincoln. By the time he took office in March 1861, seven slaveholding states had seceded from the Union. When the Confederacy demanded that Union troops surrender forts in Confederate states, Lincoln refused to give them up, acting against the advice of his cabinet. In April Confederate forces attacked Fort Sumter, South Carolina. Congress was not in session, but Lincoln acted swiftly, issuing a call for 75,000 volunteers to join the Union army and suspending habeas corpus (the right not to be imprisoned without trial). Until July 4, when Congress met, Lincoln effectively conducted the war alone.

Abraham Lincoln, photographed by Mathew Brady in 1864. William Herndon, Lincoln's law partner, described him as often looking "woe-struck."

Commander-in-chief

Lincoln was equally decisive as commander-in-chief of the Union forces. General Winfield Scott's war strategy known as the "Anaconda Plan," advised defeating the Confederacy by means of a blockade. Lincoln accepted some parts of the plan, but insisted on invading the South at multiple points. This set a pattern for Lincoln as commander-in-chief: He listened to his generals but made his own decisions. He was not blinkered by formal training and applied his intelligence devising strategies that often contradicted the military textbooks. He became one of the U.S.'s most able commanders-in-chief.

Lincoln's ideas about how the war should be fought brought him into conflict with many of his generals. He removed McClellan from command following his failure to pursue the retreating Confederates after the Battle of Antietam (Sharpsburg) in September 1862. It was a bold move, since McClellan was popular. Lincoln fired several more generals who failed to carry out his ideas.

Chief executive and party leader

Lincoln was chief executive officer of the government. Unlike Confederate President Jefferson Davis, Lincoln resisted the temptation to become involved in too much detail. A good judge of character, he chose able men to head the major departments and then usually left them alone.

The Republican Party was barely five years old when Lincoln took office. He worked hard to keep the party together throughout the war. He knew he needed the support of Congress and the public to win the war and

Curriculum Context

Students may be expected to understand the strains within the Republican Party during the Civil War.

Lincoln's appointees

Lincoln made some excellent appointments. For example, he selected William H. Seward for the important post of secretary of state. Seward initially believed Lincoln to be unintelligent and unfit for the presidency, but Lincoln overlooked this personal slight. Seward became Lincoln's most trusted adviser and did an outstanding job as secretary of state. Lincoln made a similarly objective choice for treasury secretary. Salmon P. Chase of Ohio disliked the president, but Lincoln knew that Chase had a good financial mind and was well connected in the banking world. Chase never got over his resentment of Lincoln, but he performed well. He resigned late in 1864, and Lincoln then appointed him chief justice. Lincoln also showed faith in Ulysses S. Grant, who began the war in obscurity, handicapped by a reputation as a drunkard. Lincoln noted that even when Grant failed, he made no excuses and kept fighting. The president rewarded Grant's persistence with increasingly important assignments. After Grant's victory at Chattanooga, Tennessee, in November 1863 Lincoln promoted him to general-in-chief of all Union armies. Together they devised campaigns that finally won the war.

to be reelected for a second term in 1864. He included former Whigs and Democrats in his cabinet and appointed men of all political colors to commands in the Union military.

One of Lincoln's greatest and most important assets was the way he interpreted his power. He was not afraid to sacrifice one-tenth of the Constitution to save the other nine-tenths. He was daring and innovative in his use of presidential power, making extensive use of executive orders. The greatest of these was the Emancipation Proclamation, which came into effect on January 1, 1863. Lincoln accepted that slavery could only be abolished by state-level action or by an amendment to the Constitution—neither of which were politically possible at that time. He justified the use of a presidential proclamation on the grounds of "military necessity," which is why it was limited to states in rebellion rather than applying to the whole country. For this reason the proclamation did not free slaves in Union territory.

An illustrated print of Lincoln's Emancipation Proclamation. With this executive order, which came into effect on January 1, 1863, Lincoln freed more than three million slaves in the Confederate states.

The war's end

Lincoln's leadership held the Union cause together through the first three years of the war. By mid-1864, with the fall of Atlanta, the tide had turned in favor of the North. He won the November 1864 election by a landslide. On April 9, 1865, he received the news of the Confederate surrender at Appomattox. He outlined his broad philosophy for the postwar reconstruction of the seceded states in his second inaugural address, stating that the Union should be reconstructed "with malice toward none, and charity for all." This task was left for others, because on April 14 Lincoln was shot by John Wilkes Booth as he attended a theater performance at Ford's Theater, Washington. Lincoln died the next day.

Curriculum Context

If you study Reconstruction, you may be asked to explain Lincoln's ideas about the postwar period and how they differed from the policies implemented by his successor, Andrew Johnson.

Longstreet, James

James Longstreet (1821–1904) was an able Confederate general who went on to become a political ally of President Ulysses S. Grant. He was unpopular in the postwar South, and his battlefield decisions were often criticized.

Longstreet graduated from the U.S. Military Academy at West Point in 1842 and fought in the Mexican War (1846–1848), where he was wounded. At the outbreak of the Civil War he resigned from the U.S. Army and headed to Richmond, where he was commissioned brigadier general in the Confederate army. He was assigned to the staff of General Pierre G. T. Beauregard and fought in the First Battle of Bull Run (Manassas) in July 1861. At Second Bull Run, Longstreet was slow to attack but distinguished himself with a counterattack that shattered the Union army on August 30, 1862.

Corps command

Following the Battle of Antietam (Sharpsburg), he was promoted to lieutenant general and given command of I Corps in General Robert E. Lee's Army of Northern Virginia. He took part in the Confederate victory at Fredericksburg, and the decisive Confederate defeat at Gettysburg. Longstreet went on to receive a severe shoulder wound in the Wilderness Campaign in May 1864, but returned to command with a paralyzed arm and surrendered with Lee at Appomattox in April 1865.

Longstreet was widely disliked in the postwar South because he joined the Republican Party and accepted appointments from president and former Union general Ulysses S. Grant. Many Southerners blamed Longstreet for the defeat at Gettysburg. He spent his later years in Georgia, where he ran a hotel and raised turkeys. In 1896 he published a memoir defending his actions at Gettysburg. Longstreet died in 1904.

Curriculum Context

If you are asked to analyze the Confederate defeat at Gettysburg, you might consider whether it was fair for people to blame Longstreet.

McClellan, George B.

George Brinton McClellan (1826–1885) rose quickly to take overall command of the Union army. He successfully created an effective fighting force from raw recruits, but his lack of decisiveness made him a poor battlefield commander.

McClellan graduated second in his class from the U.S. Military Academy at West Point at the young age of 20. He was immediately able to make his mark in the Mexican War (1846–1848), after which he returned to West Point to teach engineering. From 1851 he conducted surveys for the construction of military installations. Frustrated with his slow progress within the army, the ambitious McClellan resigned his commission in 1857 to became chief of engineering for the Illinois Central Railroad. By the start of the Civil War, he was president of the Ohio and Mississippi Railroad.

Return to the army

At the outbreak of the war McClellan joined the Ohio Volunteers and in May 1861 was appointed a major general in the regular army. As commander of Union forces in the Ohio Valley, his instructions were to hold on to western Virginia (later West Virginia) for the Union. He secured the region by mid-July, having actually encountered little resistance, and was being talked up in Northern newspapers as the "Young Napoleon of the West."

In the wake of the Union rout at First Bull Run he was the obvious choice to replace McDowell in command of the demoralized Union troops south of the Potomac. With the press and an adoring public behind him, by November 1861 he had managed to elbow the elderly general-in-chief of the army, Winfield Scott aside. So in just a few short months the young ex-captain had risen to command the entire U.S. Army.

Napoleon

Napoleon Bonaparte (1769–1821) was a French general who had conquered most of Europe and become celebrated as one of history's greatest military commanders; in 1804 he made himself emperor of the French.

General-in-chief

McClellan quickly showed the mixture of positive and negative qualities that made him such a baffling figure. His first achievement was to create, name, and organize the Army of the Potomac. Through the winter of 1861–62 he put in 18-hour days drilling troops and boosting morale. In this role he showed an almost comical self-importance, revealed in letters to his wife. While puffing himself up, he was scathing about the administration, including President Lincoln, whom he dismissed as "the original gorilla." More serious, though, was his reluctance to use the army he had created to confront the enemy in battle. It was not until April 1862 that Lincoln persuaded McClellan to send the Army of the Potomac out to fight.

Unfit for command

When McClellan did commit his army to real fighting, he proved unfit for battlefield command. Throughout the Peninsular Campaign (April–July 1862) he made repeated calls for reinforcements despite vastly outnumbering the enemy. After the Union defeat at the Second Battle of Bull Run, McClellan had the good fortune to see Confederate General Robert E. Lee's battle plan for Antietam (Sharpsburg). Even with that advantage he could only manage an inconclusive result in the battle. His failure to pursue the defeated Confederates seemed to demonstrate his lack of stomach for battle and gave the president the excuse he needed to strip McClellan of command.

Political career

McClellan was sidelined for the rest of the war. He tried politics, challenging Lincoln for the presidency in the election of 1864. He was heavily defeated and resigned from the army the same day. At the end of the 1870s he served as governor of New Jersey, then spent his time traveling and writing. He died in 1885.

General George B. McClellan at the height of his career. He was popular with the public, and there was wide disbelief in the North when Lincoln removed him from command in late 1862.

Curriculum Context

If you are asked to list the most important battles of the war, Antietam should probably be included.

McDowell, Irwin

General Irwin McDowell (1818–1885) was one of the least successful Union commanders. He led the Union army to defeat in the first battle of the war, at Bull Run (Manassas) on July 21, 1861, and was then relegated to corps command.

McDowell graduated from the U.S. Military Academy at West Point in 1838. When the Civil War began, he was appointed brigadier general and given command of the Union troops south of the Potomac. McDowell commanded Union forces in the first major battle of the war, at Bull Run (Manassas) where Confederates scattered Union troops and forced them to retreat.

Defending Washington

After the defeat McDowell was relegated to command of I Corps and charged with defending Washington while McClellan, who replaced him, began the Peninsular Campaign. By early July 1862, the Confederates had stopped McClellan's attempt to capture Richmond. Confederate General Robert E. Lee turned his attention north to target Union forces, including McDowell's corps. On August 29–30 the corps took part in a second battle at Bull Run Creek, which turned into a Union disaster. McDowell, who commanded the largest corps in the battle, was criticized for not using his large force effectively .

The end of McDowell's career

After Second Bull Run (the Union lost 16,000 men, the Confederates 9,200), McDowell faced accusations of failing in command. A court of inquiry cleared him, but his career in the field was over. He had desk duties for the next two years. McDowell continued to hold high positions in the U.S. Army for some years after the war. He spent his last working years as a park commissioner in San Francisco and died in 1885.

Desk duties
Administrative tasks, as opposed to service in the field with the army.

McPherson, James

McPherson (1828–1864) became the highest-ranking Union officer to die in Civil War combat when he was shot at the Battle of Atlanta in July 1864. McPherson had risen to become an able corps commander in the Army of the Tennessee.

Curriculum Context

The story of McPherson and Hood is a good illustration of the division the war drove between friends and families.

McPherson attended the U.S. Military Academy at West Point, graduating first in his class in 1853. John Bell Hood, a future Confederate general, was a great friend of his in the same class. Hood was on the opposite side at the Battle of Atlanta, where McPherson was killed.

Grant's chief engineer

In 1862 McPherson became Ulysses S. Grant's chief engineer in the successful campaign to take Forts Henry and Donelson in Tennessee. He remained chief engineer during the battles at Shiloh, Tennessee, and Iuka, Mississippi, and was promoted to major general in October 1862. In January 1863 he was given command of XVII Corps in the Army of the Tennessee. His corps played a central role in the campaign to take the Mississippi port of Vicksburg.

Atlanta campaign

On March 12, 1864, McPherson took command of the Army of the Tennessee. In spring and summer 1864, he took part in Sherman's Atlanta campaign through northern Georgia. Sherman was irritated at his caution when he failed to attack the rear of the Confederate army at Snake Creek Gap, but McPherson felt he needed more troops. Later in the campaign Sherman repeatedly used McPherson's army to outflank strong Confederate defensive positions. During the Battle of Atlanta, when Union and Confederate armies clashed to the east of the city on July 22, 1864, McPherson was shot in the back. The ball punctured his lung and passed out of his chest, and he died soon afterward.

Outflank

To pass around the side of an enemy line.

Meade, George G.

General George Gordon Meade (1815–1872) led the Union Army of the Potomac to victory at the Battle of Gettysburg in July 1863. A brave and conscientious leader, Meade had an explosive temper that could make his men wary of him.

Meade entered the U.S. Military Academy at West Point, graduating in 1835. After working as a civil engineer, he rejoined the U.S. Army in 1842 and fought in the Mexican War (1846–1848). When civil war broke out, he was made brigadier general of volunteers and given command of a Pennsylvania brigade. He participated in General George B. McClellan's Peninsular Campaign in spring 1862 and the Seven Days' Battles at the end of June, where he was seriously wounded. He was not fully recovered when he commanded his brigade at the Second Battle of Bull Run. He was promoted to major general of volunteers and commanded a division in the disastrous Union defeats that followed at Fredericksburg and Chancellorsville.

Gettysburg

President Lincoln appointed Meade commander of the Army of the Potomac in June 1863. Meade found himself up against Confederate General Robert E. Lee's Army of Northern Virginia. At Gettysburg he showed great tactical skill, and after a titanic struggle Lee withdrew, his army shattered. Meade received a congressional thank-you for his success. He remained in command of the Army of the Potomac for the rest of the war. But when General Ulysses S. Grant was made general-in-chief of all Union forces in March 1864, Meade found himself effectively demoted and subject to Grant's orders. In August 1864 Meade was promoted to major general in the regular army and after the war remained in charge of various military departments until his death from pneumonia in 1872.

Curriculum Context

You should be familiar with Gettysburg as the most decisive battle of the whole war.

Mosby, John S.

John Singleton Mosby (1833–1916), sometimes called the "Gray Ghost," led a band of partisan rangers during the Civil War. He and his men operated in an area east of the Blue Ridge Mountains that became known as "Mosby's Confederacy."

Mosby was born in 1833 in Powhatan County, Virginia. While at the University of Virginia, he was involved in an argument with a fellow student and shot him. After seven months in jail Mosby was pardoned in 1853 and began studying law. After qualifying, he joined the bar, married, and settled in Bristol, Virginia.

Scouting for Stuart

When Virginia seceded and was accepted into the Confederacy, Mosby enlisted in the army. Sent almost immediately to serve in the Shenandoah Valley, Private Mosby reported for duty with the 1st Virginia Cavalry Regiment, which was commanded by Lieutenant Colonel J. E. B. Stuart.

Stuart and Mosby got along well, and Stuart made it a practice to assign the young private difficult scouting missions to gain information about the enemy. After soldiering with Stuart in the Shenandoah Valley and Richmond campaigns of 1862, Mosby resigned from the army and formed a unit of partisan rangers in northern Virginia. Partisan rangers were irregular troops who—in April 1862—were authorized to fight independently behind enemy lines by the Confederate government.

An illustration from *The Illustrated London News* of January 1865 showing a small party of Mosby's Rangers assembling in the Blue Ridge Pass, Shenandoah Valley. Many of Mosby's raids were carried out in rugged terrain like this.

Mosby's Rangers

Mosby's unit grew until the Confederate government designated it the 43rd Battalion Virginia Cavalry. Most people called it the "Mosby's Rangers." As the rangers' leader, Mosby planned and executed raids on Union outposts in northern Virginia counties. His rangers frequently served in raiding parties and melted back into the local populace when their work was done. From 1863 to 1865 Mosby is estimated to have captured more than 1,000 Union prisoners, more than 1,000 horses, weapons and ammunition, and hundreds of thousands of dollars in U.S. currency. While Mosby's exploits caused a great deal of trouble for Union troops stationed near Washington, D.C., he caused little or no diversion of troops or resources from the fighting fronts. Unwilling to surrender with Robert E. Lee, Mosby disbanded his partisan rangers on April 21, 1865, 11 days after Lee's surrender at Appomattox.

After the war Mosby prospered, becoming friends with various U.S. presidents who secured positions for him, including ambassador to Hong Kong. Returning to Virginia in his old age, Mosby died in May 1916, one of the most famous figures of the Civil War.

Curriculum Context

Mosby would be an interesting subject for students asked to describe the influence of an individual on the course of the conflict.

Famous Raids

Two of Mosby's raids serve as examples of his daring. The raid of March 8, 1863, cemented his celebrity in both North and South. After leading 29 of his men on a ride behind enemy lines to Fairfax Court House, only a few miles from Washington, D.C., Mosby found and captured Union General Edwin Stoughton, commander of the garrison in the area. Mosby plus his men, the general, 33 other prisoners, and 58 captured horses were safely back in Warrenton by dawn.

The 1864 "Greenback Raid" was equally audacious. In the predawn darkness of October 14 Mosby's Rangers waited for a Union passenger train on the Baltimore and Ohio Railroad just west of Harpers Ferry, Virginia. The rangers displaced some rails, bringing the locomotive to a halt. They then relieved the guard of $173,000 in U.S. currency before setting the train on fire. The raid brought operations on the railroad to a halt for some time.

Pope, John

John Pope (1822–1892) served with distinction in the Union army, commanding the Army of the Mississippi and then the Army of Virginia. However, after defeat at the Second Battle of Bull Run (Manassas) he was relieved of his command.

John Pope graduated from the U.S. Military Academy at West Point in 1842, and fought in the Mexican War (1846–1848) He was promoted to captain in 1856.

Mississippi campaign

In July 1861, shortly after the outbreak of the Civil War, Pope was appointed brigadier general of volunteers. Supported by a naval flotilla under Andrew Foote, in early 1862 Pope captured New Madrid and Island No. 10 in the Mississippi River, opening up all the upper half of the Mississippi to Union forces. As a result of this successful campaign he was promoted to major general and given command of the Army of Virginia.

Flotilla
A naval unit consisting of two squadrons of small warships.

Second Battle of Bull Run

Pope came up against "Stonewall" Jackson at Cedar Mountain on August 9, 1862. Pope's forces withdrew toward Manassas Junction, but Jackson reached the town first, destroying the Union supply depot. Pope moved to attack Jackson on August 29, but Generals Robert E. Lee and James Longstreet had marched to Jackson's aid and hit Pope's left flank. The battle was a complete Confederate victory, and Pope was forced to retreat. He lost 14,500 men in the battle, while the Confederates lost 9,500. The Second Battle of Bull Run was a great Southern victory. Pope blamed his defeat on his officers. President Lincoln sympathized with him, but still relieved him of his command and sent him to the West to campaign against Native Americans. There he remained until he retired in 1886. He died on September 23, 1892.

Supply depot
A key base for storing supplies to be shipped to armies in the field.

Porter, David D.

David D. Porter (1813–1891) was one of the outstanding Union naval figures of the Civil War. He came from a distinguished naval family; he and his father were unique in having five navy ships named in their honor.

Porter was the son of a great hero of the War of 1812, Commodore David Porter. By the time he joined the U.S. Navy as a midshipman in 1829, the 16-year-old David Dixon Porter was an experienced naval hand.

Porter saw action in the Mexican War (1846–1848); but it was the Civil War that gave him the chance to shine. He was given command of USS *Powhatan* and took part in attempts to reinforce Fort Pickens off the Florida coast immediately after the Confederate attack on Fort Sumter in April 1861. The following year he teamed up with his foster-brother, David G. Farragut, in Farragut's triumphant campaign to capture New Orleans and the lower reaches of the Mississippi River.

Farragut
Read Farragut's story on page 41.

Vicksburg Campaign

In October 1862 Porter assumed command of the Mississippi Squadron, where he made a vital contribution to General Ulysses S. Grant's Vicksburg campaign, which ended in victory in July 1863. Porter received the official thanks of Congress for this and was promoted to rear admiral. In 1864 he commanded the naval side of the unsuccessful Red River Campaign. Porter ended the war on a high note, commanding the North Atlantic blockading squadron, and in January 1865 he led the largest U.S. fleet ever assembled to that time in the capture of Fort Fisher, North Carolina.

Squadron
An organization of ships including two divisions of a fleet.

After the war he became superintendent of the Naval Academy, and after the death of Farragut in 1870 he succeeded him as Admiral of the Navy. He died in 1891.

Quantrill, William C.

William Clarke Quantrill (1837–1865) was the most infamous guerrilla leader in U.S. history. His cruel and brutal tactics made him feared by civilians and soldiers alike, yet to his supporters in the South he became a folk hero.

When war broke out, Quantrill, born in Ohio, adopted the Southern cause and, with a small band of men, started to make attacks on the Missouri–Kansas border.

Guerrilla warfare

Guerrilla bands in Kansas, supporting both sides, used terror tactics that had no parallel elsewhere. Among these groups Quantrill's Raiders gained a particularly notorious reputation. After capturing Independence, Missouri, in August 1862, Quantrill was given a captain's commission and he styled himself a colonel.

Atrocity in Lawrence

After murdering 12 unarmed Union men, Quantrill and his men were declared outlaws by Union authorities. For aiding them, some of their wives and sisters were arrested and placed under guard in Kansas City. Five of them died when their building collapsed on August 14, 1863. Quantrill blamed the Union commander and sought revenge. He assembled 450 men and at dawn on August 21 led them into Lawrence, Kansas, a pro-Union stronghold. Quantrill's orders were to "kill every male and burn every house." In three hours the Raiders murdered 182 men and boys, many of them dragged from their homes to be butchered in front of their wives and children, and set fire to about 200 buildings.

Quantrill was now a marked man. In June 1865 during a raid in Kentucky he was shot. He died soon afterward in a military prison in Louisville, aged 27.

Guerrilla

Fighting through ambush, sabotage, terror raids, and assassinations.

William C. Quantrill, whose small band, known as Quantrill's Raiders, became notorious for the savagery of their guerrilla attacks against Union soldiers and sympathizers.

Scott, Winfield

When war broke out in April 1861, 74-year-old Lieutenant General Winfield Scott (1786–1866) was the U.S. Army's general-in-chief. He was responsible for the creation of the Union's first strategy to defeat the Confederacy.

Scott spent most of his life as a professional soldier. His nickname, "Old Fuss and Feathers," came from his love of military ceremony. By 1841 he was a major general and the Army's general-in-chief. He led a brilliant campaign in the Mexican War that brought victory for the United States in 1848. He ran as the Whig candidate in the 1852 presidential election, but was unsuccessful. During the secession crisis of early 1861 Scott advised President Lincoln to surrender Fort Sumter, South Carolina, to the Confederates, but Lincoln rejected the idea. Scott's choice of fellow Virginian Robert E. Lee to lead the Union army was also controversial. Lee turned down the offer and joined the Confederacy.

Whig
A member of a political party that was formed in about 1834.

Scott's war strategy

Scott believed most Southerners were loyal to the Union and could be persuaded away from the Confederacy, but not if the Union waged a war of conquest. In May 1861 he proposed a strategy to defeat the South known as the Anaconda Plan. It relied on a naval blockade of Southern ports and control of the Mississippi River to squeeze the Confederacy out of existence. Since many in the Union wanted a rapid advance south with the capture of the Confederate capital, Richmond, the Anaconda Plan was rejected.

Anaconda
A large South American snake that kills its victims by constricting, or squeezing, them to death.

Scott's age and increasing ill health led him to retire in October 1861. He died in May 1866, having lived to see the defeat of the Confederacy, brought about partly by the capture of the Mississippi and a naval blockade, which formed part of his Anaconda Plan.

Sedgwick, John

John Sedgwick (1813–1864) was a leading Union general who was in the thick of the fighting throughout the Civil War, until he fell victim to a Confederate sharpshooter near Spotsylvania on May 9, 1864.

John Sedgwick attended the U.S. Military Academy at West Point, graduating in 1837. He fought in the Second Seminole War in Florida, which ended in 1842, and a little later with distinction in the Mexican War (1846–1848). As a major in the U.S. Cavalry, Sedgwick was involved in keeping order in "Bleeding Kansas" in the late 1850s.

Curriculum Context

Students studying the hardening of attitudes before the war began should study the conflict between pro- and anti-slavery settlers in Kansas in the 1850s.

Battlefield service

"Uncle John," as he was affectionately known, served as a major in the Union army and was promoted to brigadier general in August 1861. He was involved in McClellan's Peninsular Campaign to threaten the Confederate capital of Richmond in the spring of 1862. Sedgwick was wounded during the Seven Days' Campaign at the end of June 1862. He was promoted to major general just in time to lead his division at Antietam (Sharpsburg), where he suffered three wounds and lost half his men. He returned to active service in early 1863 as a corps commander of the Army of the Potomac. He was involved in a bruising encounter with Robert E. Lee at Salem Church during the Union defeat at the Battle of Chancellorsville, and his corps was held in reserve at Gettysburg.

Sniper

An expert rifleman who targets specific individuals.

In early May 1864 Sedgwick's IX Corps survived a surprise attack on the final day of the Wilderness (May 6), then moved on to fight at Spotsylvania. His final words were allegedly that the enemy "couldn't hit an elephant at this distance." The next instant he fell dead from a sniper's bullet that hit him under the left eye.

Seward, William H.

William Henry Seward (1801–1872) was a likely candidate for the presidency in 1860, but he lost the Republican nomination to Abraham Lincoln. As Lincoln's secretary of state during the Civil War, Seward helped secure Union victory.

Seward trained as a lawyer and moved to Auburn, New York, in 1820. Western New York was a center of social reform, and it was there that he forged his antislavery views and joined the Whig Party. He served as governor (1838–1842), and in 1849 he was elected to the Senate.

Republican Party

Senator Seward spoke out against slavery, calling the differences between free and slave states an "irrepressible conflict." He joined the Republican Party in 1855, and many thought that he would be president. But Republican leaders opted for the less outspoken Abraham Lincoln as their candidate. Seward was crushed, but campaigned vigorously for Lincoln. Once in office, Lincoln appointed Seward secretary of state.

During the secession crisis of early 1861 Seward sought alliances with Southern Unionists in the hope that the Union could still be saved. Once war began he focused his efforts on preventing Britain and France from recognizing the Confederacy.

On the evening of April 14, 1865, Lewis Payne made an attempt on Seward's life as part of John Wilkes Booth's assassination plot against Lincoln. Seward survived and served out the remainder of his term under President Andrew Johnson. During Reconstruction he supported a lenient policy toward the defeated Confederate states. Although he oversaw the purchase of Alaska from Russia in 1867, he steadily lost influence. Seward resigned in 1869 and died in 1872.

Curriculum Context

Students might be expected to understand the effect of the choice of Lincoln rather than Seward as leader on the development of the Republican Party.

Shaw, Robert Gould

Robert Gould Shaw (1837–1863) was the colonel of the 54th Massachusetts, the first black regiment in the Union army. A child of privilege, born to one of the nation's wealthiest families, Shaw gave his life in the cause of racial equality.

Raised largely in New York City, Shaw spent much of his youth drinking and gambling. He spurned his parents' strong commitment to abolition and displayed little interest in their wealth. In 1861 he was a college dropout, working in his uncle's firm in New York.

Command of a black regiment

The Civil War was to reveal Shaw's talents as a soldier. In the 7th Regiment New York State National Guard, and later in the 2nd Massachusetts Infantry, Shaw demonstrated bravery in battle and leadership in camp, rising to the rank of captain. In early 1863, under pressure from African Americans who demanded the right to join the fight against slavery, President Lincoln authorized the formation of black regiments. Governor John Andrew established the 54th Massachusetts Infantry, made up largely of free blacks from the Northern states, and invited Shaw to take command as colonel. At first he refused but he reconsidered and took up his new command in February 1863. Refusing to allow the 54th to be used as a mere public relations tool, Shaw insisted that the men be trained, armed, fed, paid, and—most important—allowed to see combat. Most black units only performed support duties.

On July 18, 1863, Shaw led the 54th in a brave but unsuccessful assault on Fort Wagner, the fortress guarding the harbor in Charleston, South Carolina. Shaw was shot and killed, along with 270 of his men. His death at age 25 made him a hero of the abolitionist movement.

Curriculum Context

The story of the 54th Massachusetts Infantry is told in the 1989 movie *Glory*.

Curriculum Context

Some curricula ask students to be aware of the experiences of black troops in the Union armies.

Sheridan, Philip H

An undistinguished early career gave little indication of the dynamic and successful role General Philip Henry Sheridan (1831–1888) would play in the Civil War. He was a masterful tactician who secured vital victories for the Union.

Sheridan went to the U.S. Military Academy at West Point in 1848 after lying about his age to get in. He graduated in 1853, after being held back a year for bad behavior. Sheridan hated the South with a passion and once claimed, "If I owned both Hell and Texas, I'd rent out Texas and live in Hell."

War service

Sheridan began the Civil War as a quartermaster but lobbied for more responsibility. He returned to the Infantry as a brigadier general in the Army of the Ohio in Kentucky, where he played a vital role in the victory at Perryville. By 32 he was major general of volunteers. He impressed General Ulysses S. Grant with an attack at the Battle of Chickamauga and Grant promoted him to chief of cavalry in the Army of the Potomac.

In May 1864 Sheridan's troops attacked Richmond and killed Confederate General "Jeb" Stuart. Sheridan took command of the Army of the Shenandoah and destroyed much of the Shenandoah Valley. In October 1864, Sheridan counterattacked a surprise Confederate attack, securing a victory that gave the Union control of the valley. Sheridan was promoted to major general of regulars. His actions through the spring of 1865, capturing 6,000 men and six generals at Sayler's Creek, helped end the Civil War.

After the war Sheridan went to Texas to force the French to leave Mexico. They did a year later in 1867. Days after finishing his memoirs, he died in 1888.

Quartermaster

An officer responsible for organizing supplies for a military force.

Mexico

The French had used the distraction of the Civil War to establish a short-lived empire in Mexico.

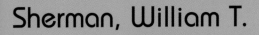

Sherman, William T.

Union General William Tecumseh Sherman (1820–1891) was one of the most ruthlessly effective Civil War commanders. His marches through Georgia and the Carolinas split the Confederacy in two and helped bring the war to an end.

Born in Lancaster, Ohio, on February 8, 1820, Sherman was one of 11 children. His father died when he was nine. Unable to cope, his mother sent him to live with Thomas Ewing, a wealthy and politically prominent neighbor, who raised him. At age 16, thanks to Ewing's influence, Sherman was admitted to the U.S. Military Academy at West Point, graduating in 1840. He spent the next 13 years as an army officer. In 1853 Sherman left the army to become a California banker.

Joining the Union army

The bank failed and in 1859 friends got him the job of superintendent of the Louisiana Military Academy, which he held when the state seceded. Sherman joined the Union army, leading a brigade at the First Battle of Bull Run (Manassas). In the fall of 1861 he was put in charge of the state of Kentucky, then the Department of the Cumberland, where his requests for more troops led to labels of "crazy." He became depressed, and asked to be relieved of his command. In March 1862 he rejoined the army, becoming commander of the Fifth Division in Major General Ulysses S. Grant's Army of the Tennessee. A Confederate army attack surprised Grant and Sherman, but Sherman did well in combat at the Battle of Shiloh (Pittsburg Landing), giving him confidence and the unwavering support of Grant.

Military governor

A soldier in charge of civil government in occupied territory.

Vicksburg Campaign

Sherman served as military governor of Memphis, Tennessee. In December 1862 Grant ordered him to assault Chickasaw Bluff just north of Vicksburg on the

Mississippi River. Grant was supposed to help but failed to show up. Sherman attacked anyway. The attack failed but Sherman played a key role in the ultimate Union victory at Vicksburg on July 4, 1863.

Command of the Army of the Tennessee

Two months later the Union Army of the Cumberland was surrounded at Chattanooga, Tennessee. Grant, Sherman, and much of the Army of the Tennessee went to its rescue. The Battle of Chattanooga was a Union success. Although Sherman mismanaged his own troops, Grant remained confident of his friend's ability. When he became Union general-in-chief in March 1864, Sherman replaced him as head of the Military Division of the Mississippi.

Advancing on Atlanta

Grant's plan for the 1864 campaign was for a concerted offensive by all Union armies at one time. Sherman

A grim-looking Sherman outside Atlanta, Georgia, in 1864. After taking the city, he ordered all civilians to leave their homes despite their protests, declaring Atlanta to be a military encampment.

Sherman's Letter to Atlanta

From General William T. Sherman's letter to the citizens of Atlanta before he took the city on September 1, 1864:

"You cannot qualify war in harsher terms than I will. War is cruelty, and you cannot refine it; and those who brought war into our country deserve all the curses and maledictions a people can pour out. I know I had no hand in making this war, and I know I will make more sacrifices today than any of you to secure peace. But you cannot have peace and a division of our country.

"You might as well appeal against the thunderstorm as against these terrible hardships of war. They are inevitable, and the only way the people of Atlanta can hope once more to live in peace and quiet at home, is to stop the war, which can only be done by admitting that it began in error and is perpetuated in pride. . . . But, my dear sirs, when peace does come, you may call on me for anything. Then will I share with you the last cracker, and watch with you to shield your homes and families against danger from every quarter."

A company of Sherman's troops, the 21st Michigan Infantry, who in all fought 13 battles in the Civil War and were with Sherman on his March to the Sea in 1864.

Curriculum Context

Students should understand Sherman's intentions on the "March to the Sea" and why the campaign was so controversial in the Confederacy.

controlled the armies of the Tennessee, the Cumberland, and the Ohio. Grant instructed him to use this massive force to do as much damage as possible. Sherman advanced on Atlanta, Georgia. He fought his way into the city but it was impossible to hold Atlanta and continue offensive operations. He decided to march to a new base at Savannah, Georgia. The Civil War had seen raids into enemy territory before, but never on such a destructive scale. Sherman believed that the operation would undermine the Southerners' will to continue by showing them that their government could not protect them. "I can make the march," he declared, "and make Georgia howl!"

March to the Sea

Sherman left Atlanta with 60,000 men on November 15, 1864. He set fire to everything—the fires wrecked part of the city. His troops continued the devastation as they marched across the state. Sherman took Savannah on December 21. He began a second march through the Carolinas on February 1. Before he could link up with Grant, Robert E. Lee's army had surrendered. In an ill-advised move Sherman reached a preliminary peace agreement with Confederate General Joseph E. Johnston. Sherman exceeded his authority. President Andrew Johnson and Secretary of War Edwin Stanton instructed him to deal only with a military capitulation of Johnston's army. This he did on April 26, 1865.

Postwar career

Despite the misstep over the terms of Johnston's surrender Sherman emerged from the war as a Union hero second only to Grant. In 1869, when Grant became president, Sherman became general-in-chief of the U.S. Army, a position he held until 1883. After retiring from the army, Sherman settled in New York City and died there on February 14, 1891.

Sickles, Daniel E.

Union General Daniel Edgar Sickles (1819–1914) was a well-known figure in political life before the war. He was one of a number of prominent Democrats commissioned as generals to widen support for the Union cause.

A Democrat, Sickles was elected to the New York Senate in 1855 and the U.S. House of Representatives between 1857 and 1861. In 1859 Sickles was acquitted of the murder of his wife's lover on the grounds of temporary insanity. He was the first person in the United States to successfully use this defense.

Popular general

Sickles supported the South's desire to secede, but he opposed its use of arms. He was commissioned a general in the Union army, but Congress refused to confirm the position because of his past. He lobbied his friends and was reinstated. A popular leader, by November 1862 he had been promoted to major general. He was given command of III Corps, Army of the Potomac, under Joseph Hooker. At Chancellorsville III Corps suffered heavy losses. At Gettysburg, General George G. Meade ordered III Corps to join the Union line along Cemetery Ridge. Sickles thought the strategy mistaken and moved his men forward. They were caught in open ground by Confederate troops, and suffered heavy losses. Sickles lost his right leg to a cannonball. He was heavily criticized for his actions.

Defending his actions

Sickles' reputation was dented by Gettysburg, and he did not command troops again. His later life was spent preserving the battlefield at Gettysburg. On his death on May 3, 1914, he was buried in Arlington National Cemetery. His leg is kept at the Armed Forces Medical Museum in Washington, D.C.

> **Temporary insanity**
> A legal defense based on the idea that someone briefly loses control of their reason.

> **Gettysburg**
> Gettysburg National Military Park was established in 1895.

Stanton, Edwin M.

Edwin McMasters Stanton (1814–1869) became secretary of war in 1862. He was a hard worker and improved the provision of supplies to the Union army. During Reconstruction he fought to improve the status of the freedmen in the South.

By the 1850s, Stanton was a well-connected attorney in Washington, D.C. Although a Democrat, he was against slavery. During the secession crisis he became an informer for the Republicans. He did not gain a place in the new cabinet, but soon began working as a legal adviser to Secretary of War Simon Cameron. When Cameron resigned in January 1862, he replaced him.

Secretary of War

Stanton had no military experience, but stamped out corruption, streamlined the chain of supply to the armies and became a trusted military adviser. He also pressed Lincoln to make emancipation a central aim and encouraged the enlistment of African American troops. He limited the freedom of the press and enforced the unpopular draft laws.

After the war Stanton feared President Andrew Johnson's timid Reconstruction policy would allow white Southerners to reimpose control over the freed slaves. He insisted on keeping martial law in place to protect the freedmen's rights. He and the Radical Republicans in Congress weakened President Johnson's control of the army. In March 1867 Congress passed the Tenure of Office Act to prevent the president firing Stanton. Johnson nevertheless fired Stanton. The House of Representatives voted to impeach Johnson in February 1868, but the Senate found him not guilty. Stanton resigned that month. He was nominated to a seat on the U.S. Supreme Court in December 1869, but died before he could take up the post.

Informer

Someone who passes on secrets to the authorities or to the police.

Curriculum Context

Many curricula ask students to consider the treatment of civil liberties such as freedom of speech by the Republican government.

Stephens, Alexander H.

Alexander Hamilton Stephens (1812–1883) was a successful lawyer and politician in Georgia before the war. He was staunchly proslavery and, following Georgia's secession, he rose to become vice president of the Confederacy.

Stephens was a leading member of the Whig Party from its founding in 1834 until its disappearance in the 1850s, after which he joined the Democrats. He stood barely 5 feet (1.52 m) tall and weighed only 100 lbs (45.5 kg). He defended slavery but opposed secession. When Georgia seceded from the Union, however, he decided to support the Confederacy.

Confederate vice president

Georgia constituents elected Stephens to the provisional congress of the Confederacy in early 1861. He chaired the committee that wrote the Confederate constitution, which he modeled on the U.S. Constitution while adding features that protected slavery and states' rights. Speaking in Savannah, Georgia, in March 1861, Stephens gained attention when he said that the Confederacy's "cornerstone rests upon the great truth that the negro is not equal to the white man; that slavery … is his natural and normal condition." His words damaged Davis's efforts to justify secession on the grounds of "states' rights." Stephens was also openly critical of Davis's war measures and chose to spend 18 months of the war based in Georgia rather than in the capital at Richmond.

After the war Stephens was imprisoned for five months, then returned to Georgia. He was elected to the U.S. Senate in 1866, but was denied his seat by the Republicans who controlled Congress. He took up his seat in the House in 1873. In 1882 he became governor of Georgia, holding the office until his death in 1883.

Curriculum Context

Students studying the outbreak of the war should consider whether there was a contradiction in Stephens' and Davis's account of the reasons for the creation of the Confederacy.

Stowe, Harriet Beecher

Abraham Lincoln once described Harriet Beecher Stowe (1811–1896) as "the little lady who wrote the book that made this great war." The book he referred to was *Uncle Tom's Cabin*, published in 1852, which described the cruelty of slavery.

Harriet Beecher Stowe was born on June 14, 1811, in Litchfield, Connecticut, the seventh child of the preacher Lyman Beecher. Her family had strong religious beliefs and thought that girls' education was very important. She was a student and then a teacher at a school in Hartford run by her sister Catherine until 1832, when the family moved to Cincinnati.

A writer from an early age, Harriet wrote stories for Christian publications. In 1836 she married Calvin E. Stowe, a professor at Lane Theological Seminary; together they had seven children. In 1850 they moved to Brunswick, Maine, where Stowe began *Uncle Tom's Cabin* in angry response to the Fugitive Slave Law of 1850, which allowed owners to hunt runaway slaves anywhere in the country and made it the public's duty to help them catch the fugitives.

Uncle Tom's Cabin was published first in serial form in the *National Era* magazine. It was an instant hit when it was published in book form in 1852, selling 50,000 copies in eight weeks. It was the best-selling novel of the 19th century and brought the horrors of slavery to a wide audience.

The novel's influence

Uncle Tom's Cabin was so influential that it has been regarded as one of the triggers of the Civil War. It told the story of Tom, a slave, and his treatment by his three owners, each representing a different type of slave master, from kind to fatally cruel. By focusing on the

Curriculum Context

The Fugitive Slave Law outraged many people in the North. You might be asked to describe its consequences: *Uncle Tom's Cabin* was one.

Curriculum Context

Some curricula ask students to assess the importance of the novel in the hardening of attitudes that eventually led to war.

dehumanizing effect of slavery on family relationships, the novel connected with the emotions of its readers. Despite its success in the North and in Europe, it was widely denounced in the South. Stowe had to defend it from critics by publishing a list of source material in support of her portrayal of slavery in 1853. She only wrote one more antislavery novel, *Dred: A Tale of the Great Dismal Swamp*, published in 1856.

Stowe went on to write many more novels, travelogues, children's stories, and theological works. She believed that education was the key to social change and in 1867 traveled to Florida to help the newly freed slaves. She continued to champion the rights of freedmen until she suffered a stroke in 1889. She died seven years later in 1896.

Freedmen

The name given to former slaves who were freed during the war or in its aftermath.

Harriet Beecher Stowe said of her bestselling antislavery novel *Uncle Tom's Cabin*, "God wrote the book. I took his dictation."

Stuart, J.E.B.

James Ewell Brown Stuart (1833–1864) was one of the Confederacy's greatest cavalrymen. His legendary scouting skills provided the Confederates with crucial information about the disposition of Union forces and their battle plans.

Scouting

Undertaking reconnaissance missions to learn about the enemy.

Curriculum Context

Stuart' could be included in a list of the great military heroes of the Confederacy, along with Robert E. Lee and Thomas "Stonewall" Jackson.

"Jeb" Stuart served with the 1st U.S. Cavalry Regiment in Kansas and Texas before the Civil War. In July 1861, as a colonel of the 1st Virginia Cavalry, Stuart led a charge that greatly helped the Confederate victory at the First Battle of Bull Run. Promoted to brigadier general, he carried out scouting duties during the Peninsular Campaign, giving General Robert E. Lee valuable information about Union positions.

Stuart's most famous exploit was his ride in June 1862 around Union General George B. McClellan's 100,000 troops camped outside Richmond, Virginia. On the three-day raid his 1,200 men rode 100 miles (160 km), capturing 165 men and 260 horses. After this, Stuart was promoted, aged just 28, to major general in charge of all cavalry in the Army of Northern Virginia. Later that summer he raided the headquarters of Union General John Pope during the second Bull Run campaign, making off with one of Pope's own uniforms and important documents.

Gettysburg

In June 1863 Stuart went on a raid in Pennsylvania and lost touch with the main army, depriving Lee of vital intelligence in the run-up to Gettysburg. He did not arrive until the second day of battle. Harshly criticized for his actions, Stuart kept in close touch with Lee throughout the fall, while continuing to harass Union troops. On May 11, 1864, Stuart's cavalry encountered Union cavalry at Yellow Tavern, outside Richmond. In the clash Stuart was shot and died the next day.

Thomas, George H.

George H. Thomas (1816–1870) was a Southerner who chose to fight for the Union. Following the Battle of Chickamauga, he was given command of the Army of the Cumberland. His greatest victory was at the Battle of Nashville in December 1864.

Thomas graduated from the U.S. Military Academy at West Point in 1840, and fought against the Seminole in 1841 and in the Mexican War (1846–1848). At the outbreak of the Civil War, Thomas was torn between conflicting loyalties. He decided to fight for the Union. This alienated him from members of his family and generated mistrust in Union quarters.

The "Rock of Chickamauga"

Thomas was sent to Kentucky as a brigadier general of volunteers and in January 1862 defeated a Confederate force at Mill Springs—the first significant Union victory in the West. Thomas made his mark on September 20, 1863, when at the Battle of Chickamauga his heroic defense saved the badly mauled Union army from a rout. Dubbed the "Rock of Chickamauga," he was given command of the Army of the Cumberland and served under Ulysses S. Grant at Chattanooga and then William T. Sherman in the Atlanta Campaign.

The fall of Atlanta in September 1864 moved Thomas into a central role. He was given the task of chasing Confederate General John Bell Hood into Tennessee. However, Grant grew impatient with his slowness and sent another general to replace him. Before this took effect Thomas launched an attack on Hood at Nashville. His crushing victory stilled criticism, and saw him promoted to major general and thanked by Congress. He stayed in command in Tennessee until after the end of the war. In 1867 he took command of the military division of the Pacific in San Francisco, where he died.

Seminole

Native Americans in Florida who fought a series of wars against the U.S. Army in the first half of the 19th century.

Curriculum Context

Chickamauga proved to be one of the decisive battles of the war.

Tubman, Harriet

Civil War nurse, scout, and Union spy, Harriet Tubman (c. 1820–1913) fled from slavery as a young woman and escaped to the North. Known as the "Moses of her people," she went on to help many other slaves reach freedom.

Harriet Tubman (née Ross) was born a slave. When she was 25, Harriet married a free African American, John Tubman. Five years later, learning that she was to be sold, Harriet fled to Philadelphia. Aged 27, she discovered her husband had been unfaithful, and left him. She then began a career as rescuer of some 300 slaves, making 19 trips to the South to lead them north. Tubman soon had a $40,000 reward on her head. Initially she led fugitives to Canada, where they did not face recapture, and where she lived for six years. In 1857 she moved to Auburn, New York, and bought a farm from Senator William H. Seward, where she cared for her elderly parents and other escaped slaves.

Civil War life

During the war Tubman became a Union scout. In July 1863 she guided troops commanded by Colonel James Montgomery on an expedition to the Combahee River in South Carolina to disrupt Confederate supply lines. During the mission she helped free more than 750 slaves and came under fire. She also spied for the Union, getting information from African Americans in the Confederacy. She nursed black soldiers and worked in a Freedmen's Hospital in Virginia. Her work was not officially authorized so she did not get a pension. In 1869 she married Civil War veteran Nelson Davis.

In 1890 Congress granted Tubman a small monthly payment. She spent the rest of her life running a home for elderly African Americans in Auburn, New York, where she died in 1913.

Curriculum Context

You might be expected to be familiar with Tubman's activities as one of the most famous "conductors" on the "Underground Railroad" that led slaves to safety in the North.

Supply lines

The routes by which armies in the field receive food, ammunition, and other supplies.

Watie, Stand

Brought up in a wealthy, land-owning Cherokee family, Isaac "Stand" Watie (1806–1871), whose Cherokee name "De Gata Ga" means "he stands," was the only Native American to become a general during the Civil War.

Watie was among a number of leading Cherokee who signed a treaty in 1835 agreeing to the removal of the Cherokee Nation to Indian Territory (now Oklahoma). A slave owner, he became the leader of a minority Cherokee faction opposing abolition. When war broke out, he became a colonel in the Confederate army. His regiment, the Cherokee Mounted Rifles, came to specialize in highly effective hit-and-run raids. Watie's men defeated Union forces at the Battle of Oak Hill, which reinforced the South's hold on Indian Territory and made Watie a Confederate hero. In the Battle of Chustenahlah on December 26, 1861, Watie's troops helped push pro-Union Native Americans out of Indian Territory. During the war Watie and his men saw action in some 18 battles, successfully tying up Union troops and preventing them from fighting elsewhere. During the war Watie attempted to take over the leadership of the Cherokee. Chief John Ross was persuaded by the Union to change allegiance in summer 1862. While he was away in Washington, D.C., Watie declared himself the new Cherokee chief, so splitting the Cherokee Nation.

His finest hour
Watie's greatest military achievement came in mid-1864. He captured a Union supply boat, the USS *J.R. Williams*, and then, at the Second Battle of Cabin Creek on September 19, 1864, a Union wagon train with $1.5 million worth of supplies. Watie was the last Confederate general to lay down his arms, only surrendering on June 23, 1865. He died six years later.

General Stand Watie's many daring raids into Union territory engaged thousands of Union troops who were badly needed to fight farther east.

Waud, Alfred R.

Alfred Rudolph Waud (1828–1891) was one of the war's leading artists. His dramatic and detailed illustrations realistically re-created the many aspects of army life for the readers of the New York Illustrated News and Harper's Weekly.

Born in London, England, Waud studied art and design before emigrating to the United States in 1850. He worked as an illustrator on East Coast publications. When war broke out, he was working for the New York *Illustrated News*. Both he and his younger brother William were sent to the war as "special artists."

A drawing of a female sutler by Alfred Waud. Sutlers were civilians who followed the armies and sold items such as food, tobacco, newspapers, and tin plates to the troops at the front.

Alfred Waud followed the Union Army of the Potomac from the first major battle of the war at Bull Run in July 1861 to the surrender of General Robert E. Lee at Appomattox in April 1865. He lived and worked among the soldiers, drawing intimate scenes of camp life as well as events in battle. He was able to capture the whirlwind pace of combat in a way photographers could not. He and Edwin Forbes were the only artists believed to be present at the Battle of Gettysburg.

Too grisly

Waud included realistic details in his drawings, and his battle sketches were sometimes thought too explicit for the general public and were changed before publication. Many of his works have a haunting quality, such as *Wounded Escaping from the Burning Woods in the Wilderness* (1864). After the war, Waud continued to work as an illustrator, traveling extensively in the South to make a series of illustrations on daily life. He died on a tour in Georgia in 1891.

Welles, Gideon

Gideon Welles (1802–1878) enjoyed a long career as a politically motivated newspaper editor before the Civil War. Appointed secretary of the Union navy in 1861, he brought drive and incorruptible integrity to his new job.

Welles's early attempts to get elected to the House of Representatives and the Senate as a Democrat failed, and he channeled his energies into crusading journalism. In 1854 he was one of the founders of the Republican Party; and the same year launched the *Hartford Evening Press*, one of the earliest and most influential Republican newspapers in New England. His unsuccessful attempt to become governor of Connecticut in 1856 brought him to the attention of Abraham Lincoln. When President Lincoln formed his carefully balanced cabinet in 1861, he appointed Welles secretary of the navy in recognition of New England and former Democrats, who, like Welles, had joined the Republican Party.

Secretary of the navy

As secretary of the navy, Welles succeeded in creating a powerful Union navy that was able to impose a naval blockade on 3,000 miles (4,830 km) of Confederate coast. The navy grew from 90 ships in 1861 to 670 in 1865, while naval personnel soared from just under 9,000 to nearly 60,000. Welles supported the ironclads, which revolutionized naval warfare. He also appointed the great naval commanders David G. Farragut and David D. Porter.

Politically, Welles was a moderate Republican. In 1868 he rejoined the Democratic Party. His diary of the war years, not published until 1911, gives valuable insights into the leading personalities of the Civil War. Welles died in 1878.

Blockade

A system of naval patrols and other defenses intended to prevent any marine trade in or out of enemy ports.

Curriculum Context

The development of the ironclads is a good example of how technological innovation in the Civil War affected future warfare.

Glossary

abolitionists Members of the campaign to make slavery illegal.

alderman A senior official in town or city government.

ambush A surprise attack launched by hidden troops who have been lying in wait.

anaconda A large South American snake that kills its victims by constricting, or squeezing, them to death.

assassinate To murder someone by sudden and secret attack.

battery An artillery unit, consisting of a number of guns and their crews.

blockade A system of naval patrols and other defenses intended to prevent any maritime trade in or out of enemy ports.

blockade-runner a sailor or ship that ran through the Union blockade of Southern ports during the Civil War.

brevet rank A promotion for an army officer to a higher rank, often as an honor just before retirement. There was no increase in pay and a limited increase in responsibilities.

brigade A military unit of around 5,000 soldiers made up of between two and six regiments. The brigade was the common tactical unit of the Civil War.

casualty A soldier lost in battle through death, wounds, sickness, capture, or missing in action.

carbine A short rifle used by cavalry soldiers riding on horseback.

cavalry Mounted soldiers; the role of cavalry changed considerably during the course of the war.

company A military unit consisting of 50 to 100 men commanded by a captain. There were 10 companies in a regiment. Companies were raised by individual states.

corps The largest military unit in the Civil War armies, consisting of two or more divisions. Corps were established in the Union army in March 1862 and in the Confederate army in November 1862.

counteroffensive An advance launched in response to an enemy offensive.

daguerreotype An early photographic process invented in France in 1839 by Louis Daguerre.

desk duties Administrative tasks, as opposed to service in the field with the army.

dispatches Written orders and reports between military commanders.

diversionary Describing a military action intended to distract the enemy from a larger action.

division The second largest military unit in the Civil War armies. A division was made up of three or four brigades and was commanded by a brigadier or major general. There were between two and four divisions in a corps.

field hospital A temporary hospital set up in tents or in adapted buildings near a battlefield.

forced march A march that is so long or made so quickly that it would normally exhaust the soldiers making it but which is militarily necessary.

freedmen The name given to former slaves who were freed during the war or in its aftermath.

guerrilla warfare A military conflict fought through ambush, sabotage, terror raids, and assassinations.

habeas corpus A legal protection against being imprisoned without trial. President Abraham Lincoln was severely criticized for suspending the right to trial in the Union during the war. President Jefferson Davis took a similar unpopular measure in the Confederacy.

infantry Foot soldiers.

inflation A rapid and widespread increase in prices.

informer Someone who passes on secrets to the authorities or to the police.

ironclad A ship protected by iron armor.

Lost Cause After the war the Lost Cause created a vision of the prewar South as a happy and harmonious society, destroyed by the industrialized and resentful North.

Medal of Honor The highest U.S. award for gallantry, introduced by Abraham Lincoln in 1862.

Mexican War The United States fought Mexico from 1846 to 1848, following the U.S. annexation of Texas.

military governor A soldier in charge of civil government in occupied territory.

Mormon War A standoff between the U.S. Army and Mormon settlers in Utah, whose laws did not fit with those of the United States.

outflank To pass around the ends of an enemy line.

partisan raiders Irregular bands of troops, authorized by the Confederate government in April 1862 to operate behind enemy lines. They wore uniforms and were paid for captured war material they gave to the government.

Peninsular Campaign A Union campaign in spring and summer 1862 that attempted to capture Richmond via the Virginia Peninsula.

Presbyterian A member of a Protestant church that follows the doctrines of John Calvin.

private The lowest rank in an army.

quartermaster The officer in charge of providing supplies to the troops.

quinine An anti-malaria medicine made from the bark of a South American tree.

Radical Republicans A group of Republicans who believed that Lincoln was too moderate in his approach to slavery, which they wanted to be abolished without compensation to slave owners.

rear guard A small unit that protects the back of a much larger group as it retreats.

Reconstruction era The period from 1865 to 1877, when the Confederate states were rebuilt and brought back into the Union.

regiment A military unit consisting of 10 companies of 100 men at full strength. In practice, most Civil War regiments were much smaller than this. Raised by state governors, they were usually composed of men from the same area. The Civil War soldier's main loyalty and sense of identity was connected to his regiment.

scouting Gathering information about the enemy through small-scale missions.

secessionist A person who supported the breaking away of the Southern states from the United States and was thus a supporter of the Confederacy.

sniper An expert rifleman who targets specific individuals.

supply depot A key base for storing supplies to be shipped to armies in the field.

temporary insanity A legal defense based on the idea that someone briefly loses control of their reason.

unconditional surrender A surrender whose terms are not negotiated but are wholly imposed by the victors.

Unionist A person who believed that the United States had to be preserved intact.

Whig Party A political party formed in 1834 to promote manufacturing and commercial and financial interests.

Further Research

BOOKS

Alexander, Bevin. *Lost Victories: The Military Genius of Stonewall Jackson*. Hippocrene Books, 2004.

Barney, William L. *The Oxford Encyclopedia of the Civil War*. Oxford University Press, 2011.

Blackman, Ann. *Wild Rose: The True Story of a Civil War Spy*. Random House Trade Paperbacks, 2006.

Caravantes, Peggy. *Petticoat Spies: Six Women Spies of the Civil War*. Morgan Reynolds Publishing, 2002.

Catton, Bruce. *The Civil War*. Boston, MA: Houghton Mifflin, 1987.

Coles, David J., et al. *Encyclopedia of the American Civil War: Political, Social, and Military History*. W.W. Norton and Company, 2002.

Cooper, William J. *Jefferson Davis and the Civil War Era*. Louisiana State University Press, 2008.

Frank, Lisa Tendrich. *Women in the American Civil War* (2 vols). ABC-Clio, 2007.

Gienapp, William E. *Abraham Lincoln and Civil War America: A Biography*. Oxford University Press, 2002.

Grant, Ulysses S. *Personal Memoirs*. New York: Crescent Books, 1995.

Harper, Judith E. *Women During the Civil War: An Encyclopedia*. Routledge, 2007.

Holzer, Harold, and Craig Symonds. *The New York Times Complete Civil War 1861–1865*. Black Dog and Leventhal Publishers, 2010.

Marrin, Albert. *Commander in Chief: Abraham Lincoln in the Civil War*. New York: Dutton, 1997.

Monroe, Dan, and Bruce Tap. *Shapers of the Great Debate on the Civil War: A Biographical Dictionary*. Greenwood, 2005.

Mosier, John. *Grant: Lessons in Leadership*. Palgrave Macmillan, 2006.

Oates, Stephen B. *A Woman of Valor: Clara Barton and the Civil War*. New York: Macmillan/Free Press, 1994.

Reynolds, David S. *John Brown, Abolitionist: The Man Who Killed Slavery, Sparked the Civil War, and Seeded Civil Rights*. Vintage, 2006.

Robertson, James I. *Soldiers Blue and Gray*. Columbia, SC: University of South Carolina Press, 1998.

Schindler, Stanley (editor). *Memoirs of Robert E. Lee*. New York: Crescent Books, 1994.

Schultz, Jane E. *Women at the Front: Hospital Workers in Civil War America*. University of North Carolina Press, 2007.

Smith, Gene. *Lee and Grant: A Dual Biography*. New York: McGraw-Hill, 1984.

Trudeau, Noah Andre. *Robert E. Lee: Lessons in Leadership*. Palgrave Macmillan, 2010.

Van Woodward, C. (editor). *Mary Chesnut's Civil War*. New Haven, CN: Yale University Press, 1981.

Wiley, Bell Irvin. *The Life of Johnny Reb: The Common Soldier of the Confederacy*. Baton Rouge, LA: Louisiana State University Press, 1980.

Wiley, Bell Irvin. *The Life of Billy Yank: The Common Soldier of the Union*. Baton Rouge, LA: Louisiana State University Press, 1981.

Winkler, H. Donald. *Stealing Secrets: How a Few Daring Women Deceived Generals, Impacted Battles, and Altered the Course of the Civil War*. Cumberland House, 2010.

Woodworth, Steven E. *Sherman: Lessons in Leadership*. Palgrave Macmillan, 2010.

INTERNET RESOURCES

These general sites have comprehensive links to a large number of Civil War topics:

http://sunsite.utk.edu/civil-war/warweb.html

http://civilwarhome.com/

http://americancivilwar.com/

http://www.civil-war.net/

http://www2.cr.nps.gov/abpp/battles/bystate.htm
This part of the National Parks Service site allows you to search for battles by state

http://pdmusic.org/civilwar.html
Sound files and words to Civil War songs

http://www.civilwarmed.org/
National Museum of Civil War Medicine

http://memory.loc.gov/ammem/aaohtml/exhibit/aopart4.html
Civil War section of the African American Odyssey online exhibition at the Library of Congress

http://valley.vcdh.virginia.edu/
The Valley of the Shadow Project: details of Civil War life in two communities, one Northern and one Southern

http://www.civilwarhome.com/records.htm
Battle reports by commanding generals from the Official Records

http://www.cwc.lsu.edu/
The United States Civil War Center at Lousiana State University

http://www.nps.gov/gett/gettkidz/soldslang.htm
Civil War slang from the site of the Gettysburg National Military Park

http://www.sonofthesouth.net/leefoundation/ebooks.htm
The Robert E. Lee Foundation digital library of books about Lee and about the Civil War generally

Index

Page numbers in *italic* refer to illustrations and captions.

H

habeas corpus 73
Halleck, Henry W. 54
Hammond, William A. 7
Hancock, Winfield Scott 55
Harper's Ferry 18
Hill, Ambrose P. 56
home front 27
Hood, John Bell 35, 57, 80, 101
Hooker, Joseph 23, 58–59, *59*
hospitals 36

I

Iron Brigade 46
ironclad 105

J

Jackson, Thomas J. "Stonewall"
6, 12, 45, 60–62, *62*
Johnson, Andrew 25, 63–64
Johnston, Albert S. 49, 65
Johnston, Joseph E. 8, 35, 66
94
journalists 52

K

Kansas 31, 86
Kansas–Nebraska Act 72
Kentucky 19, 20
Knoxville, siege 24
Ku Klux Klan 44

L

Lanier, Sidney 67
Lawrence, Kansas 86
Lee, Robert E. 11, 18, 34, 50,
59, 61–62, *62*, 68–71, *69*,
70, 81
"Light Division" 56
Lincoln, Abraham 6, 10, 11, 20,
38, 49, 52, 63–64, 72–75,
89
and McClellan 78
Little Bighorn, Battle of the 46
Longstreet, James 76
"Lost Cause" 39, 71
Louisiana Military Academy 92

M

Manassas 79
March to the Sea *94*
Massachusetts Anti-Slavery
Society 37
McClellan, George B. 23, 74,
77–78, *78*
McDowell, Irwin 8, 30, 79
McPherson, James 80
Meade, George G. 55, 81
Medal of Honor 26
Mexican War 8, 17, 20, 32, 39,
40, 46, 48, 55, 58, 65, 68,
76, 77, 81, 84, 87, 88,
101
Mississippi 33, 42
Mississippi River 84, 85, 87
Mobile, Alabama 42
Mormon War 21
Morse, Samuel 13, 14
Mosby, John Singleton 82–83
Mosby's Rangers *82*, 83
"mud march" 23
Murfreesboro, Tennessee 43

N

New Orleans 25, 42, 85
New York Tribune 52
nursing 7, 29, 36

O

Ohio Valley 77
Overland Campaign 50–51,
51, 71

P

partisan rangers 82-83
Peninsular Campaign 22, 58,
61, 78, 88, 100
Perryville, Battle of 19
Petersburg 24, 26, 71
photographers 15, *15*
photography 13–16
Pierce, Franklin 33
Pinkerton, Allan 53
Plains Indians 31
poetry 67
politics 6

Polk, Leonidas 35
Pope, John 45, 84, 100
Port Hudson 6
Porter, David D. 41, 85
Pottawatomie Creek 18

Q

Quantrill's Raiders *86*
Quantrill, William C. 86, *86*

R

Radical Republicans 96
raids, cavalry 83
Reconstruction 38, 75, 89, 96
Reconstruction Bill 64
Republican Party 6, 72, 74, 76,
89, 105
Richmond 10, 22, 28, 33

S

Savannah, Georgia 94
Scott, Winfield 68–69, 73, 77,
87
scouting 102
secession 73, 89
Second Battle of Bull Run 61,
70, 76, 79, 81, 84
Sedgwick, John 88
Senate, U.S. 27
Seven Days' Battles 47, 81, 88
Seward, William H. 74, 89
Sharpsburg (Antietam), Battle
of 56, 78
Shaw, Robert Gould 90
Shenandoah Valley 6, 45, 61,
91
Sheridan, Philip H. 91
Sherman, William T. 48, 51, 80,,
92–94
Shiloh, Battle of 29
Sickles, Daniel E. 95
Siege of Petersburg 55
Sitting Bull 31
slavery 18, 25, 37–38, 52, 63,
89, 98, 99, 102
South Carolina 27
South Dakota 31
South, the 76
spies 8, 12, 53, 102

Who I Am

Who I Am

poems by Julius Lester
photographs by David Gahr

The Dial Press, New York

The following six photographs were taken by Julius Lester:
"The Keeper," third, fourth, and sixth photographs; "Where
Whales Sing," both photographs; "Four Haiku," last photograph.

Library of Congress Cataloging in Publication Data
Lester, Julius. Who I am.
I. Title.
PS3562.E853W5   811'.5'4   73-15447
ISBN 0-8037-8758-8

For Moses Asch

"If anybody ask you who I am,
Tell 'em I'm a child of God"

—AFRO-AMERICAN SPIRITUAL

The Keeper

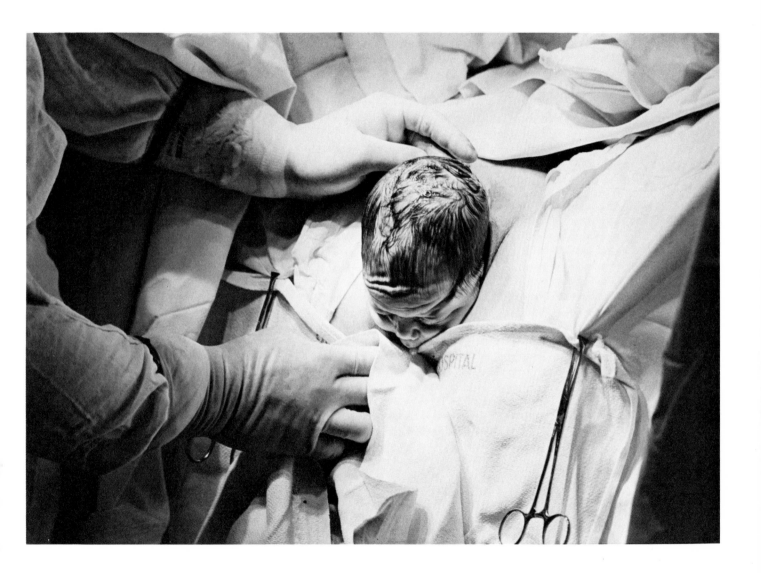

Why are the first years of our lives
someone else's memories?

My parents remember –

the infant staring wide-eyed, the
child experimenting with the world and
beginning to know itself.

Like a diver searching the ocean floor
for sunken Spanish galleons and gold doubloons,

I look for the child from whom I grew,
but even the stains of my tears
have rusted.

So, I keep the memory
of my children and
one day will give them
this treasure

If they'll accept it.

Where Whales Sing

When I want to see my face,
I use the sky as a mirror.

When I forget who I am,
I lick my dog's nose.

When asked my name,
I say "Tree."

If no one understands,
I do not explain.
Words are just lines on a map,
too often mistaken for the road

Which leads to the
Silence where whales sing, wild grasses cry
and I lie curled
in the armpit of
God.

New York

"How can anyone
raise children in New York?"
(Nervous chuckle.) "It's a great place
to visit, but
I wouldn't want to live there."

the tourist,
garlanded with cameras,
sees (with postcard eyes)
the streets layered in dirt/paper/broken glass/dogshit/sleep-
     ing drunks and Unidentified Fallen Objects
the buildings lining sixth avenue like skinny mountain ranges
the weary-faced tenements huddled back from the streets
     like bowery winos dreading yet another winter.

the stranger sees the peopled streets
but not the lives
which cannot be toured –

the old women, numbers etched on their wrists, sitting
on benches near grant's tomb

young black men perched on grimy stoops like
   ashanti warriors on golden stools

young girls whose smiles come from where the sun lives.

new york is people –

each one with his/her own face . . .

each one a snowflake of crystalline fragility
melting all too soon.

Sylvia

though I loved her,
sylvia walked into the sea.

though I
loved her, she gave her
self to the indifferent sea.

and the fish nibbled those breasts
which had filled my mouth
while the crabs ate
the dark eyes that had sung me praises.

I loved sylvia

sylvia did not

and she walked into the ocean sylvia
walked into the sea.

If only she had drowned my love,
too.

Four Haiku

Autumn afternoon:
Drinking tea,
I listen to the rain.

I tried
to hear the silence:
Spring morning.

Ah! The cawing of
The crows at dawn
This winter morning.

On this summer day
I have no doubt that
I will live forever.

Love Affair

I carry my body with me
as if it were battered luggage,
or old newspapers to be discarded without soiling my hands.

I never touch my body
and say, I like you,
Body. (When it itches, I scratch. When
it is dirty, I wash it.) I
live in my body as if it were
a foreign country.

Ah, to lie
naked
with my legs open to the sky
and let the sun's rays
(like hands)
caress me.

I think
I will have a love affair
with
my body.

Everything is Somebody?

Everything we use
is somebody's job.

(Ergo: EveryThing is
somebody?)

who puts the stick-
um on envelopes/stamps and
band-aids? who makes toothpicks/
toothpaste/toothbrushes and
toilet paper? Do people who work
in dog food factories ever taste it?
And somebody somewhere every
day puts seats in cars. (Imagine that.)
What do people look like
who make paperclips/rubber bands/erasers/
lipstick/hairbrushes/toilet bowls/
(do men or women make brassieres?/soap/
picture frames/How do they get
the ink in ballpoint pens? Do you know
how many people it takes to make
a napkin?) Every-

Thing is
SomeBody('s
job)

Imagine that.

When I was Young

When I was young
love was hard kisses and sweaty palms
and I thought I would love her always (whoever she was)
because love (I thought)
stretched into forever.

When I was young
love was the smile
between warm-night thighs,
the spring-spun silk of budding breasts,
and desire fluttering like
butterfly wings.

But when I grew up
(and that took thirty years)
I learned
(slowly and with many tears) that
love
is the recognition of self
through the gift of another,

A perpetual
l
  e
    a
      p
        i
          n
            g

to my
Self

(I am
therefore I
love)

Love is a mirror
in which I see
a ME (!)
who never lived
until there was a
YOU (!!!)

Loving is not
I need you
but
I give you.

Loving is
wanting the other
to be him/her-
self, to know that —

The world is a toy
a plaything
a bauble
a game –

And one soars
to him/herself . . .

for love is the beginning
from which
all else
proceeds.

Who I Am

I am who I am.

Must I give a name to that?
Must I say

I am black
I am a man
I am a writer?

Those are statements of fact
(the sky is blue. water is wet. snow is cold.)

But what is black?
    Not even the color of my true love's hair
        (which is red)
What is a man?
    The figment of a penis' imagination
What is a writer (doctor/lawyer/Indian chief)?
    What you put in the space of income tax forms
        that says OCCUPATION_____.

So who am I?

I am
who I am
and if that leaves you perplexed,
will you accept that

I am
you?